Love is what's needed, Ditto is what's said.

Ronald Thompson

Copyright © 2023

All Rights Reserved

ISBN: 979-8-391-13471-8

Dedication

I dedicate this book to my wife, whose love and inspiration inspired me to write it. Thank you for believing in me and for allowing me to dream.

Acknowledgment

To Genay, my love.

You have been the most influential person in my life. From day one, you've been nothing but genuine. Love was a slow process for me, yet you were patient and understanding as I figured it out. I am thankful to have you in my storybook called Life.

Thank you for teaching me how to receive love, and more importantly, thank you for showing me how to give love.

Thank you, Mom.

Writing this book was therapeutic for me, in the sense that I just set out to write from my character's perspective, and came to a realization of what it was like for her growing up.

It all begins with her, Melvina Brown, who raised me by herself. My mother was a single parent just trying to raise a young black male, as she was still figuring out life for herself. I love you, Mom.

About the Author

Originally from Cincinnati, Ohio, Ron is a huge Ohio State football fan who now resides in Georgia. Ron is the proudest of his family and extended family.

Ron began writing children's books in 2020 during COVID as a hobby and has written 20 books, with six of those books to be published this calendar year. Ditto is his first book to be published.

Preface

Justin is wracked with the ghosts of his past, and his childhood trauma. When Ivy, a beautifully breathtaking nutritionist, joins the gym Justin works at, cupids arrow finds him unexpectedly. Justin, still holding on to his past, continues to shun love, not allowing for lasting connections. He struggles from listening to his heart, by giving love a chance, to remaining detached, and emotionally unavailable. Justin seeks the help from his best friend and a Therapist to navigate the uncharted waters of emotions.

Contents

Dedication i
Acknowledgment ii
About the Author iii
Preface iv
Chapter 1: Justin and Amber 1
Chapter 2: Present Day 5
Chapter 3: The Pool Fiasco 13
Chapter 4: Dancing Bachata 18
Chapter 5: Commitment Issues 29
Chapter 6: The Date 45
Chapter 7: The Club 61
Chapter 8: Maternal Affection 68
Chapter 9: Unable to Say the Words 74
Chapter 10: A Decision to Make 85
Chapter 11: Art and Ivy 91
Chapter 12: No More Ditto 106
Epilogue 133

Chapter 1: Justin and Amber

"I was 17, and it was my senior year. I remember being very excited," Justin said, with his eyes closed, his expression turning wistful as he remembered the past.

The school bell blared as kids started to fill the halls. One of them was Justin, who grabbed his books from his locker just as Amber, his girlfriend, walked up and kissed him on the cheek.

"See you at the party later tonight," she said, and he grinned.

"Okay," he said, closing his locker door.

"I love you!" Amber said softly, her eyes wide and dripping with honesty.

"I love you, too," Justin said, slightly embarrassed.

Amber walked away, and Justin's best friend, Miguel, caught up with him, along with four other teenagers, all joking and laughing.

"Dude… did you say you love her?" one of the guys asked. "You never tell them that." He playfully hit Justin on the arm, and the other guys started to tease him. When they left, Miguel chuckled.

"Don't listen to them, lover boy," he said sarcastically.

"Shut up!" Justin said, a scowl marring his otherwise handsome face. "Just be on time to pick me up for the party. I'm asking Amber out to prom tonight."

Justin was eager to see how things would go. He had been dating Amber for a while and was certain she would say yes.

Filled with anticipation, he rushed home and began getting ready for the party. His mother thumped up the stairs, stood in the doorway, and said, "Mow the yard and put together the bookshelf in my room."

Justin looked up from his perch on the bed, a slight scowl at the edge of his lips. "I'm getting ready for the party. Can I do it tomorrow?" he asked.

"I want it done today," his mother said impatiently. "And don't step a foot outside this house without doing it."

Justin groaned but hurled himself off the bed, doing what his mother had said. He quickly finished cutting the grass and then put together the bookshelf, his movements sluggish and exhausted.

Then he hurriedly got dressed, fingers fumbling with haste, and walked down the stairs, stopping when he saw his mother sitting on the couch in front of the TV.

"Bye, I'm heading out," he told her.

She didn't turn to acknowledge him. "You put the bookshelf in the wrong spot. I wanted it over here," she instructed, pointing at a random corner in the living room.

Justin simply stared at her, his face crumbling in hurt and pain. He hesitated for a second, but hearing Miguel honking from out front, he quickly left the house, putting on a fake smile for Miguel as he slipped into the passenger's seat.

The party was in full swing. Teens were laughing, talking, dancing, having a good time, and just enjoying the carefree feeling of youth. The music was upbeat and refreshing, but Justin did not stop, walking with purpose as he pushed past the teens, looking for Amber.

When he made his way to the living room, he saw a crowd of people standing around a closet, cheering whoever was inside. Curious, he pushed past the throng of people and made it to the front.

His heart shattered when he saw Amber, with her hair all over the place, making out with a random buff guy while the other teenagers egged them on.

Suddenly, Amber's eyes met his and widened in shock. She pushed the guy she was kissing out of the way, making the kids around them laugh. She stared at Justin, her expression flooded with guilt, and reached out, but Justin had already turned around.

Devastated, Justin pushed through the crowd and ran toward the car, with Miguel running after him. He was distraught but did not want anyone to notice how heartbroken he was.

Miguel ran after him, stopped beside the car, and kneeled over. His breath came in massive pants. "That was quite disappointing," he complained. "Did you see the arms on that guy?! He was huge! Like incredibly huge!"

"Yo chill," Justin said, slipping into the car and holding his head in his hands, feeling a headache coming on.

Miguel went around to the driver's seat and sat inside the car, turning the ignition on.

"Sorry, bro, but he was packing," Miguel admitted. "Even I would date him."

Justin slammed the car door shut, his jaw clenched in anger. "I need to get in shape, bro. And I will never tell anyone I love them ever again!" he said as he made a promise to himself.

Chapter 2: Present Day

Justin opened his eyes as he lay on the couch in his therapist's office, looking up at the ceiling. There were numerous brightly colored photos on the walls and the desk.

"That was pretty traumatic. How did that affect you?" the therapist asked, his voice placating.

"It was a smack in the face," Justin admitted. "Made it harder to open up to anyone. I shut down even more and went back to being the person I was trying to escape."

"And who was that?" his therapist wondered out loud. He leaned back and peered at him over the edge of his golden-rimmed glasses.

"Someone who is heartless, emotionally detached, and insensitive toward the feelings of the women I was dating. It made me not want to open up to anyone, male or female. And to be honest, i'm not even sure if I'm going to be able to continue to speak to you today."

With that, Justin paused, second-guessing himself, and then sat up. "You know? This may be a bad idea. I don't even know why I came here today."

"Ain't it obvious?" his therapist asked with a little chuckle. "You're in love."

"Love!? Love has shat on me. First in the form of my mom and then my high school girlfriend. What has love gotten me? Nothing. The only two women I've ever opened up to have crushed me."

The therapist opened his mouth to say something, but Justin cut him off. "Love is not for me," he declared as he laid back down and carried on with his story.

THE WORD 'DITTO '

In Uptown Cincinnati, Justin stood in the gym, training one of his current clients, and thought to himself, 'I'm quite proud of myself,' I've accomplished so much in the past ten years. I am now the number one personal trainer in the Cincinnati area. I'm in high demand in and out of the gym. I even worked on my physique, and now, I'm built like a brick house. I'm the go-to person for everything personal training.'

He looked at his client, instructing him till his timer beeped and the session ended. "Great job with today's workout," *he encouraged.* "Just five more minutes of cool down, and I'll see you tomorrow!"

Justin walked away from his client, heading to a room with a door plaque that read 'Head Trainer.' He knew he was not the biggest guy in the gym; his genetics had failed him there. But he was still in great shape and had boundless amounts of stamina.

Looking at himself in the mirror, he flexed his body, admiring his abs before he sat down at his desk. Just as he had made himself comfortable, Miguel barged through the door, an arrival that made Justin scowl.

"Where the hoes at?" Miquel yelled. "Yo, last night was crazy!"

Justin laughed at Miguel's expressions as they reminisced about the night before. They had been out partying, dancing, and having a good time. That would not have been Justin's kind of scene a few years ago pre-work out bod, but things had changed. He was now a man on a mission, partying and dancing regularly. And on this night, one of his side chicks told Justin, "I love you," making him panic.

He stumbled and stared at her while she waited for his response when he came to a realization. "Ditto!" he finally choked out.

'I don't have to say I love you, and I will still get what I want,' he had thought, and when the girl looked up at him, he smiled.

"Ditto! Yeah, ditto, baby," he said out loud.

Justin shook his head, clearing his mind of any thoughts of last night. "Well, tonight will be even better," he promised Miguel. "Holla at me later. I gotta talk to the old man."

"No doubt," Miguel said. "I got Miss Lynn at nine. She's the ultimate-" he said before he broke his sentence off and grinned at Justin.

"Short body caddy!" the two said in unison before breaking into a bout of laughter.

"You know? That's my thing," Miguel said. "I like fat booties and short body caddy! Simply means she's stacked... and thick!"

Justin laughed and shook his head, standing up and making his way out of the office. Miguel followed close behind. "What can I say?" he said. "I like big butts, and I cannot lie."

"No doubt," Justin said. "See you later, bro."

Miguel walked out of the office, going to the gym's reception to see his client, and Justin made his way to the boss' office.

Justin entered the office without knocking and called out to Ron, his boss, who was in the process of fishing out an M&M from the huge pack he kept hidden in his desk.

When Justin opened the door, he fumbled, hurrying to hide it. Justin looked at Ron with his hand in a bag of M&Ms and gave him an accusatory glance.

Ron immediately said, "Cough drops! I have a cold," as he loudly started fake-coughing.

"Boss, it's 90 degrees outside," Justin said suspiciously, crossing his sculpted arms over his buff chest.

Ron coughed harder, trying to lie his way through it, just when an M&M fell from the bag and rolled over to his feet. His expression turned into one of guilt, and he immediately kicked it away, hoping Justin had not seen it.

"It's seasonal allergies," Ron said adamantly.

Justin shook his head, choosing not to dwell on the topic. "Right. Anyway, boss, when are you going to promote me to a manager at the LA location?"

Ron immediately became more serious. "Does a bear shit in the woods and wipe his ass with a white rabbit?" he asked metaphorically.

There was a brief pause as they stared at each other. Ron waited for an answer while Justin stared at him in confusion, not knowing where the conversation was heading.

"Exactly, you need to get your shit together," Ron continued.

"I bring business here!" Justin argued, taking a few steps closer to Ron's desk. "People come here to be trained by the best. I'm not only the top trainer here;

I'm the top trainer in the tri-state!" He sat down in the chair in front of Ron's desk, aggravated.

"You know what I'm referring to. It's all this poonanny chasing in the gym," Ron said.

"I'm a young man," Justin justified. "I can't help it if the ladies can't keep their hands off me."

"You cannot keep running around here like a chicken without a head, chasing these women. You're gonna miss out on a great opportunity. Get yourself together, and you will have so many women on you that you will have to beat them off with a shovel," Ron advised.

"The phrase is 'beat them off with a stick,' not shovel," Justin corrected.

"Stick, shovel; I don't give a damn. Use both of them," Ron grouched, signaling for him to leave.

Justin left Ron's office, disappointed, and Miguel made his way toward him. "How'd it go?" he asked, noting Justin's deflated body language.

"He's still trippin', but soon, that promotion is going to be mine, and we'll be off to LA, where all the ladies play," Justin said, straightening himself.

One of the staff members turned up the TV volume because of the mention of local kid Trey Harris. Justin and Miquel turned to listen.

"The University of Cincinnati football team seems to have themselves the projected #1 draft pick in running back, Trey Harris!" the TV announcer was saying. "And from what I've seen in today's game, that projection is correct."

"I'm with you," the second TV announcer agreed. "He was as advertised. He was outstanding today!"

Justin turned away from the TV. "I would love to train a kid like that," he told Miguel wistfully. "That would definitely confirm my status as a top-tier trainer and get me a ticket out of here."

"Hey, you never know!" Miguel said. "It could happen."

Natalia, their coworker, walked up to them as they continued to look at the TV screen. "Your 9 am body assessment is waiting in your office," she told Justin.

He nodded. "Thanks. How are things with you and Jane? She's not still insecure, is she?" he asked.

Natalia grimaced. "Yes. She doesn't trust anyone, honestly, especially trainers. She thinks they're all dogs," she said.

They both looked at the person in question and saw that she was already looking at them suspiciously as if she knew they were talking about her.

"Wow, I can't believe people still believe stuff like that," Justin said, and Natalia rolled her eyes in silent agreement.

They said their byes, and Justin walked toward his office. As soon he had closed the door behind him, his 9 am client pulled him into a kiss. He reciprocated, making out with her in the middle of his office. Nothing about the situation was unusual for him.

"I love you," his client said.

"Ditto," Justin replied, pulling her in for another kiss.

Twenty minutes later, she left his office, her hair all over the place and her clothes disheveled. Justin saw her out and saw Miguel training his client from across the gym.

Miguel was trying to focus on the task and not gawk at how his client's butt was stuck in the air. He tried his hardest to retain some semblance of professionalism.

Justin laughed. "I'll see you later," he mouthed before leaving the gym. He had big plans for the night.

Chapter 3: The Pool Fiasco

Justin sat on the couch in his therapist's office. His chest inflated with a certain confidence and pride

"Believe it or not, I pride myself on being a professional. I believe in providing the utmost in customer service," he declared, and his therapist chuckled, shaking his head amusedly.

"And the word 'ditto'?" he asked.

"It just felt natural," Justin explained. "No commitment, so no expectation. And I'm still rewarded in the end."

The therapist kept his face impassive as he wrote 'Detachment' on a yellow memo notepad.

Justin was getting dressed for the night. He looked around and smiled when he saw that his apartment was completely equipped to cater to the possible needs of any woman, furnished with all essentials - from shower caps to curling irons.

He buttoned his shirt and then called Miguel after he was ready.

"What up?" Miguel asked when he answered the phone, sounding distracted. He was playing a video game.

"Yo, meet me at the gym at around 11ish. I have a surprise," Justin said.

"The gym?" Miguel wondered. "For what? To train?!" His words were punctuated with frustration because his character in the game was killed. "Maldita sea!!"

"No fool," Justin said impatiently. "Come ready with trunks... or don't come at all."

"Ooh okay. Now you're talking!" Miguel exclaimed. Then his tone changed, and he shouted at the game. "Take that, puta."

Justin rolled his eyes and said, "Out," before quickly hanging up the phone.

A few hours later, he pulled up to the gym with two women to find Miguel waiting at the entrance.

"Man, what took you so long?" Miguel asked, walking toward the car as soon as Justin pulled up.

"Don't worry. I got you," Justin said. He walked over to the back of the car and opened the door, letting the two scantily clad women sitting inside get out.

"Damn, short body caddy!" Miguel whispered to Justin.

"Yes, my friend," Justin clarified with a proud nod. "That is definitely a short body caddy." Then he unlocked the gym, and they all walked in. He pointed to the girl's locker rooms and looked at the women

meaningfully. "Go ahead and get changed, ladies. Miguel and I will do the same and join you both by the pool."

"Yo Jay, you sure?" Miguel asked. "If Ron catches us in here, he will be beyond pissed."

"You worry too much. I got this," Justin assured him before turning on the music in the pool area. The two of them entered the pool and waited for the women.

Finally, they trampled out, both wearing two-piece bathing suits. The tall woman removed her top before joining them in the pool. Once completely submerged, she removed her remaining clothes and threw them out of the pool.

Justin bit his lip and said, "You look amazing."

She smiled and pushed herself against him with a mumbled, "I love you Zaddy!"

"Ditto," Justin said, pulling her closer.

Miguel tried to get her friend to do the same, but all she could talk about was the kids she had left at home, making him roll his eyes.

The two couples were just rounding second base when, unbeknownst to them, Ron pulled up outside the gym. As soon as he walked inside, his girlfriend in tow, he realized what was happening.

"Baby, go wait for me in my office while I handle something. I won't be too long. This will just take a second," he told his girlfriend, his eyes fixed on the pool's door.

Then he turned on the lights and cut off the music; his face etched into a scowl. The group looked shocked, wondering what had happened. Miguel and his new companion, who had been twerking on the side of the pool, stopped mid-twerk.

Justin recognized Ron's silhouette through the frosted glass door and urged the women to leave. The tall woman jumped out of the pool, exposing her backside as she ran while trying to cover herself with a towel. Afraid of what Ron would do, Miguel scurried away with the girls.

"Not you! Just the girls!" Justin exclaimed in frustration as he watched Miguel run off.

He sighed and got out of the pool, approaching Ron, who had already caught sight of the two women and Miguel.

"Sorry, this won't happen again," Justin said.

"I thought the broiler room incident was the last time-" Ron said, reminding him of the time he had caught Justin making out with a girl.

"Or maybe the basketball court incident-" he continued, talking about the time he had walked into a similar situation in the recreational room.

"Or even the time in the spinning class," he had caught Justin with two girls.

"I can expl-" Justin began to say, but Ron cut him off.

"This is the last time, Justin. I can't trust you. I can't promote you. This is exactly the kind of foolery that has you here, being average, instead of in LA, being your own boss."

Justin nodded, trying to find a way out, but in the end, he just gave up and walked off, exiting the gym.

Ron called his girlfriend, and they made their way toward the pool. However, Ron shook his head, suddenly reminded of the woman who had been in there, completely naked. "I know that girl with all that ass left some booty residue here. Let's get in the Jacuzzi, mama," he told his girlfriend, and she giggled as they shared a passionate kiss.

Chapter 4: Dancing Bachata

"Sounds like you have a little trouble being a one-woman guy," Justin's therapist said with a slight chuckle.

"I did. I was young and dumb and not making any excuses, but it's what I was taught from an early age from the older guys coming up," Justin justified.

"And what was that?" his therapist asked. "What were you taught?"

Justin sat up and leaned toward the therapist, fixing him with an intense look. "You know how a young lion cub instinctively knows how to hunt because it's in his DNA?"

"Yes," his therapist said.

"Well then, you know, as men, we instinctively know how to hunt… women. It's in our DNA." Justin paused, weighing his words carefully and adding, "But not in some crazy psycho way."

They both laughed, and he continued.

"Nah, I'm just saying it means nothing to me. It meant nothing to me to date and move on to the next girl. I was told never to tell them you love them."

The therapist raised one eyebrow and asked, "Justin, tell me about your relationship with your mother. What was it like while you were growing up?"

"There was no relationship other than me being the child and her my mother," Justin confessed. "My mother wasn't emotionally there when it came to me. No hugs, no kisses, and no telling me I did a great job, only what I did wrong. I felt like a stranger in my house. And because of that type of upbringing, it eventually rubbed off on me, you know?"

"I think I understand," the therapist said. "Please continue with the story."

Miguel knocked on Justin's door and peeked his head inside to see Justin with his head on his desk.

"Is the coast clear?" he asked tentatively.

Justin looked up at him and rolled his eyes. "It is for you. I told the girls to leave, not you. I took the heat for both of us."

"Sorry, man. I got nervous," he said, taking in the scowl on Justin's face.

"It's cool," Justin said, a smile pulling at the corner of his lips.

They both laughed, and then Miguel said, "Anyway, your 8 am appointment is here for her training session. I think it might be a good session. Her name is Ivy."

He winked at Justin, shut the door, and left. Justin smirked, understanding what he meant, before gathering himself and walking toward the front desk.

Sure enough, a beautiful, tall Latina woman stood at the front desk. He was taken aback by how stunning she was.

"Hello, I'm Justin," he said, approaching her and introducing himself with an easy smile. "I'm the head trainer. For you, that just means you're in good hands."

"Oh, am I?" Ivy asked, one eyebrow raised, but Justin did not respond, leading the way.

They both entered Justin's office, and she took a seat. Justin pulled out a packet of paperwork and a business card and passed them to Ivy across the desk.

"What's this?" Ivy asked.

"A little paperwork," he said. "This lets me know exactly what your goals are and where to begin. The business card is for any questions you may have later."

"Oh, okay," she said, filling out the paperwork. Justin examined her face and body closely, his eyebrows raised when he noticed her excellent physique.

He hesitated before saying, "I hope this doesn't come off wrong, but you seem to be in great shape already."

Ivy looked up and flashed him a quick smile. "Thank you, I try," she said. "Professionally, I am a nutritional consultant and run my own business, but it's my love for dancing that keeps me in shape."

"That's fantastic!" Justin exclaimed. "I knew something was up. I have a good eye."

"From all the awards on the wall, I guess you know what you are talking about," Ivy said with a grin.

Justin nodded. "Yeah, I know a little something, something," he said humbly. "I like the fact that you are a nutritionist. It would be great for businesses to tie in training tips for your clients."

Ivy nodded enthusiastically. "That was exactly my thinking!" she said.

Justin and Ivy moved to the central part of the gym, performing several workouts, the chemistry between them was so palpable it could have been cut with a knife, but neither wanted to risk anything. After the workout was over, he brought her a water bottle and a towel.

"You did great. I guess that Jane Fonda tape was worth the buy," he told her, and she laughed, making him grin.

"You got jokes," she said. "Jane Fonda tapes... Ok... what gave it away? The jumping jacks or the high knees?"

"Neither," he said wittily. "I would have to say it was the outfit."

He was right. Her workout outfit resembled something that seemed to be straight from Jane Fonda's wardrobe.

They both laughed, and then he said, "No, but really. You did terrific. That was a really good session."

"Thank you," she said bashfully. "I had fun."

"Hey, I don't know what you have going on later, but we have appreciation member night on Tuesday nights here at the gym. And I wanted to know if you would like to come and have some pizza?" Justin offered.

"Wait a minute," she said, catching on. "You guys give your clients a beat down and then offer them pizza?"

Justin laughed, realizing how absurd it was for a fitness gym to offer pizza. "Yes, but no. You don't have to eat the pizza. It's a great way to connect with other members," he told her.

"Um, I don't know," she said with a shrug.

"You can get potential leads for your business. As a matter of fact, every member you see stuffing their face with pizza… feel free to go hand out a business card," he joked, making her chuckle.

"Okay, I will attend," she said with a gentle smile. "But with business cards in hand."

"Great!" Justin said excitedly before realizing his tone was too bright and correcting himself. "I mean, cool. See you later."

Ivy smiled and turned to leave the gym before realizing she had not provided a contact number.

"I didn't leave you my number," she said, calling out to Justin.

He held up the clipboard and showed her her contact information, muttering, "It's right here."

Ivy laughed and playfully rolled her eyes. "Creepo," she said, and Justin smiled as she walked away.

Miguel dashed up to him as soon as she was out of sight. "Yo, what happened?" he demanded. "Did she give you her number?"

"Yeah, sort of…" Justin said, trailing off.

"Huh?" Miguel asked.

"I got it off her profile, but she was cool with it," he elaborated, and Miguel shook his head.

"That's definitely creep status, Jay," he pointed out.

Justin shrugged. "She's a baddie, and I'm definitely feeling her energy," he said.

"Where is she from?" Miguel pressed. "DR, PR, Colombia. What is she?"

"Don't know," Justin said shortly. "Why does it matter?"

"Because there are different levels of crazy," Miguel whispered conspiratorially.

Justin's forehead creased with concern. "What do you mean different levels of crazy?" he questioned.

"Latinas are the sweetest, most beautiful, loving, amazing, evil, psychotic creatures you will ever meet," Miguel clarified.

"NOOOO," Justin explained, disbelief marring his tone. "Why is that?"

"Not for certain. But me personally? I think it's just a crazy gene papi. It's in their blood," he said.

"What?!" Justin yelled.

"You'll be okay," Miguel said, lowering his voice and looking somber. "Maybe."

"I heard that!" Justin proclaimed.

"Yo, I got you. I will be your little Latina information center to help you navigate a great experience, so you don't get cut," Miguel reassured.

"Cut?!" Justin asked.

"Yes, but don't mind that right now. We don't have a lot of time since you are seeing her tonight, without a background check or any knowledge about whether she's loca or not," Miguel said before lowering his voice again. "Stupido."

"We're just meeting here for pizza tonight," Justin clarified, convinced it could possibly not be that bad.

"You never know," Miguel mused. "So, we're gonna do a little crash course on things to say and not to say. Probably more to do and not to do. Like no sudden moves to ensure you don't get cut."

"You joking, right?" Justin asked, one perfectly arched brow raised.

"Yes." Miguel hesitated. "Well, no. I need you to focus. Quick question, did you eat any beans today?"

Justin was extremely confused. "Not today," he said.

"Good," Miguel said with a nod of approval. "Make sure not to eat any if you guys are getting together to eat."

"Why not?" Justin demanded.

"Because beans on top of beans will make your culo sing," Miguel explained.

"Culo?!"

"Yes, culo. Your butt. Your anus. Your pooper," Miguel replied.

Justin's face crumpled in disgust.

"Anyway," he said, thinking of a subject change. "Yo, I seen this couple dancing on TV the other day. They were doing some dance called um...ba...bashutoe. It was really sexy. Teach me how to do that, my Latina information center?"

"It's called 'bachata'," Miguel stated. "And I'm your guy. I'm well versed in bachata. I gotchu."

He closed the office door and then started to move the desk back, lining it against the wall and making a lot of noise.

Then he turned on the music and held his arms out.

"Come here," he said. He placed Justin's right arm in the air and positioned his left arm on his back. "Follow my lead. I'll play you, and you'll play her."

"Yo, I'm not playing the girl," Justin said, scowling.

"Do you want to take the lead?" Miguel demanded impatiently. Justin stared at him blankly and silently grinned because he knew he was being difficult.

"Just be quiet and let me lead my darling," Miguel said.

Justin gritted his teeth.

"Don't push it," he growled.

Miguel ignored him and pulled Justin closer, placing his hands on his hips.

"Loosen your hips and stare into my eyes like you want me," he said before emitting a fart.

Justin wrinkled his nose in disgust.

"Did you fart?" he asked.

"Yes," Miguel said honestly. Justin held back a gag. He rolled his eyes and reluctantly followed Miguel's lead, doing everything he asked. Initially, he kept stepping on Miguel's feet and had a hard time, making a lot of noise. At one point, they started bickering loudly, but soon, Justin started getting the hang of it, just enough to even take the lead and dip Miguel.

"My guy, you got it," Miguel encouraged. "Just keep practicing when you get home before going out."

"Good lookin' out, fam!" Justin said, and they fist-bumped.

He grabbed his jacket and left the office, Miguel following close behind. As soon as they exited, everyone turned to look at them, having heard the *suspiciously loud noises that had been coming from the office.*

They stopped and stared at the crowd before Miguel said, "Never mind them."

As Justin opened the door to leave the gym, Miguel gave one last piece of advice that could potentially help him on the date, "By any means, do not say anything bad about J. Lo. She's our Queen B. We will fight you about Jenny."

"Fool! Get out of here," Justin said, rolling his eyes and walking to his car.

Miguel opened the gym door and shouted, "No sudden moves and yes to all things 'Jenny from the block'!"

He began to hum 'Jenny from the block' as he turned to go inside the gym, hoping Justin's 'hang out' would go well.

Chapter 5: Commitment Issues

Justin danced around the office with his imaginary partner, glancing at the therapist occasionally.

"Wow! She must be really special. Was this the first time you felt like this out of all your other partners?" the therapist asked.

"Yes. I experienced a lot of firsts with Ivy. She's the first person that made me want to open up," Justin confessed.

"You said 'made you want to,' suggesting you didn't open up to her yourself," his therapist pointed out.

"No, I didn't. Not at first," he said as he continued dancing.

"Believe me. I wanted to. I struggle with trying to express what I'm feeling. It doesn't come naturally. Heck, it was a big deal coming here," he hesitated, taking a deep breath. "Like I told you, I didn't grow up in a household where emotions were shared."

"I get it. Your hesitancy about wanting to open up after being bottled up for so long has to be difficult for you," his therapist said.

"It's definitely a work in progress," Justin admitted.

"Your friend Miguel really has your back?" the therapist continued.

Justin continued to hum bachata.

"Yes. Always have. That's my dog," he said.

"Have you ever told Miguel how much you appreciate him?" his therapist asked. "And that you love him?"

"Well, no," Justin said, slight irritation seeping into his tone. "Guys don't talk like that. He knows."

"You guys have been friends since high school, and you've never told him you love him and how much you appreciate his friendship?" his therapist wondered out loud. "You know, Justin? I hope you get to a healing point in your life before it's too late, before you meet an emotionally available person. Because if you keep holding on to the past, you will cause them to pull away."

Irritated by what the therapist just alluded to, Justin stopped dancing, threw himself on the couch, and started to reflect, thinking about the night he had gone out on his first date with Ivy.

Justin got dressed, folded his sleeves, and headed to the gym, anxiously waiting for Ivy to arrive.

Everything was slow and uninteresting at the gym, even though Justin was occupied mingling with two members. That was, till Ivy walked in, caught sight of him, and smiled. Justin met her at the door, looking extremely handsome.

"This place is really jumping tonight. Throwing pizza all around and knocking chairs over," Ivy said sarcastically, looking around and noticing that it was practically empty. She looked breathtaking, and Justin struggled to look away from her.

"Oh, that's funny," he commented with an eye roll, and they both chuckled. "It's never like this. It's usually packed. I don't know what happened today."

"You guys didn't change the pizza toppings did y'all?" Ivy joked, and Justin laughed.

He quirked a brow and said, "Do you wanna get out of here? I know a little restaurant not too far away. We could check it out?"

"Sure, that would be cool," Ivy agreed.

"Okay, I'll meet you there," he said.

A little while later, Justin pulled up to the restaurant, and a valet attendant took his keys, mumbling, "Hello, Mr. Tyrese-"

"Nooo!" Justin groaned, cutting him off.

The attendant raised his brow questioningly and tried again. "Mr. Ditty?"

"Noooo!" Justin said.

"Mr. Cassanova?"

"No, no, and no. You've never seen me here before, and my name is Justin!"

"Justin?" the attendant said under his breath, annoyed. "Don't even look like a Justin."

Justin ignored him and walked into the restaurant. The host immediately greeted him with a smile and said, "Hello, Mr. Michael B Jordan!"

Justin groaned, feeling a headache coming on.

"No. Look, I've never been here before. Please call me Justin."

The host looked confused.

"What do you mean? You're a regular here, although with different women and various names."

Justin was exasperated.

"Mind your business," he said. "Here's $10 to pass the message along to the other waiters that my name is Justin."

"Justin?" the host asked, looking at the money, seeming entirely unamused.

"Yes. JUSTIN!"

"Did you say $50?" the host plied, a slight smirk playing at the edge of his lips.

Justin's eyes widened.

"That's ridiculous! For $50, you better pass it along to all the waiters and your momma," he said sarcastically.

"Excuse me?" the host asked, offended.

"Nothing!" Justin said hotly. He pulled out the money and handed it over to the host.

"Thank you, Justin. I will pass the message along!"

"Thank you," Justin said sarcastically. "Now, where is my date?"

When the host looked confused, Justin started describing her height using his hands.

"She's a little-"

"Yes, she's a little cutie with a fat booty," the host finished for him, looking bored.

Justin shook his finger at the host, slightly perturbed by what he had just said.

"See, I can't right now with you!" he muttered, just as his eyes caught sight of Ivy sitting at one of the tables. When she saw him walking toward her, she stood up and greeted him with a hug.

"I hope I didn't have you waiting too long?" Justin asked amiably, his annoyance melting away.

"Not at all," she assured him.

"How are you feeling after our session?"

"Not too bad. That wasn't your best, was it?" she asked, and he laughed, shaking his head.

"Oh no. It was just a little something to gauge your condition," he said honestly.

The server walked over to the table, looked at Justin, and pretended to not recognize him.

"Hello, I'm Landon. I will be taking your orders tonight. Is this your first time here?" he asked, and then, unable to keep up the pretense, winked at Justin.

"Yes!" Justin said quickly.

"Great, please take your time looking over the menu," Landon chirped. "What can I get you both to drink?"

"Two waters with lemon," Justin said immediately before looking over at Ivy. "Is that okay?"

"That will be fine. Thank you," she said politely as the waiter walked away.

"What are you getting?"

"I always order the same thing when I come here," Justin said and then quickly corrected himself. "I mean…when I come to places like this. Steak and potatoes."

"I think I'll get the Ropa Viejah," Ivy declared, having thoroughly scanned the menu.

"What's that?" he asked.

"It's stewed shredded beef with veggies, rice, and beans," she told him.

"Beans?! Huh…" Justin wondered, remembering what Miguel had told him.

"We will have to do a little extra cardio tomorrow, but it's so worth it. I never get to eat like this anymore," she said with a small smile.

"Sounds good. I've never tried a Spanish dish before, so I'll give it a try," he said.

"I promise you, you will enjoy it!" she vowed.

The server came back to take their orders and placed the drinks on the table. When he left, Justin asked, "Ivy, how did you become a nutritional expert?"

"Well, obesity and high cholesterol run in my family, and I wanted a different narrative for me. So initially, it was just about educating myself and my loved ones. I started to see the difference it made in just my family, and it made me want to help more families. So, I decided to start my own nutritional consulting practice."

"That's wonderful," he said honestly. "How is business?"

"Just okay right now. I'm missing something," Ivy said, and Justin nodded, understanding where she was coming from.

"Enough about me. What made you want to become a personal trainer? You know most people think trainers make out with their clients," Ivy said, and Justin snickered nervously, alarmed at how uncomfortably close to the truth she was.

"Yes, I keep hearing that," he said shortly.

"So, why a trainer?" Ivy pushed.

"My story isn't as inspiring as yours," Justin said, gritting his teeth, thinking back to the time he had watched his first love make out with a buff guy in a closet. "I simply just trained for various sports and loved the results I got, so I became a trainer. Somewhere along the way, I loved seeing the transformation in the people I was training. They would come in with low self-esteem, but once the transformation starts happening, you see a different person on the outside and, more importantly, on the inside. It made me feel accomplished."

"It feels good making a difference in someone's life by simply doing what you love to do," she said, agreeing. "How long have you lived in Cincinnati?"

"I've lived here all my life. Grew up downtown and moved to the suburbs in junior high school. What about you?" he asked.

"I've been here close to a year. I moved here to care for my mom, who passed away a few months ago," she said.

"So sorry to hear that," he said.

She brushed away his sympathy with a casual, "It's okay, really. And thank you. I've just been so busy; I haven't been able to take in the city."

"What?!" Justin asked, a quick smile pulling at his lips. "I'm your guy!"

"Really?" she paused. "Okay. We'll see," she said, and Justin smiled.

"So, who's your favorite rap artist, Justin?"

"Pac, of course!" Justin blurted.

"Yes, Pac! Mine too. Who is your favorite female singer?" Ivy asked excitedly.

"Jennifer Lopez. Hands down. I would go so far as to say she is in my top three most amazing people. God, Pac, and Jennifer, and not in that order. Me personally? I would put Jennifer first," trying to emphasize his love for J. Lo like Miguel had advised him to.

Ivy snorted.

"Okayyy," she said.

The server arrived with their food, and they shared a hearty meal, laughing, and realizing they had quite a lot in common.

Eventually, the plates were taken away, the last bites swallowed, and Justin smiled at Ivy.

"That was great," he said. "Thank you for the recommendation."

Ivy looked up at him and noticed he had some food on the corner of his lip. She wiped it away, not realizing how close she was to him. They stared at each other for a few intense moments before Ivy looked away and said, "Yes, I told you, you were going to enjoy it. I grew up making this dish from scratch with my Abuela."

"It was great," Justin said. "I have to learn more about you and your culture."

Ivy smiled.

"I'd like that," she said. "Excuse me while I go to the restroom."

As Ivy got up, the server returned and placed the bill on the table.

"I can pay it right now. Hold on," Justin said, paying up and leaving a five-dollar tip.

"Ninja, this is an $100 tab. So, P. Diddy, Tyrese, Casanova, Mickey Mouse- whoever you may be, I need my coins, or Miss Thang here is about to find out

who you really are. And I'm sure that would be cause for no nightcap for you tonight, sir! So, what's it gunna be?" the server demanded sassily.

Justin pulled out his wallet and placed another $5 on the table, making the server place his hands on his hips and say, "Try again, honey."

Annoyed, Justin pulled out a $1 bill, and the server said, "No nightcap tonight, sir!"

Irritated, he decided to go all in but then saw Ivy rounding the corner.

"Is everything okay?" she asked, stopping at the table.

Justin readjusted his position and pleasantly said, "Oh, yes. I was just paying this server for his fine service."

He handed the server a $10 bill.

"Yes. Everything is fine."

He stood up and placed his arm around Ivy's waist to guide her away from the table, glancing back at the infuriated server who was occupied with cleaning their table.

"Casanova, my ass!" the waiter mumbled under his breath. "Don't play with me about my coins! It's expensive to look this good."

Ivy and Justin walked out of the restaurant and waited for the valet.

Justin turned to her and asked, "Where's your car?"

"I took a taxi," she told him. "It's always hard to find parking midtown."

"I'm so sorry," he said. "I didn't know. I just assumed you drove to the gym. You could have driven with me. Please allow me to take you home."

"Are you sure?" she asked, taken aback by his kind gesture. "I can grab a taxi."

"No, it's the least I can do for you for agreeing to hang out on such short notice," he insisted, and Ivy smiled.

When the car pulled up, he opened the door for her like a gentleman and let her step inside. He turned around, to the valet attendant holding his hand out for a tip. He swallowed back his curses and handed over a $20 bill, aware that Ivy was watching.

"Thank you, sir," the valet said, with a grin on his face.

Justin glared at him over the top of his car and slipped him the middle finger.

"Fucker," he mouthed, but out loud, he said, "Thank you. Have a goodnight!" Then he got into the driver's seat, and they drove off.

Justin took Ivy around the Cincinnati area, pointing out the sights and singing along to the music on the stereo. Eventually, he said, "Okay, enough for tonight. Let me get you home. Where to?"

"I'm at 707 Clark Street, downtown. On the westside," *she said, and he entered the address into the GPS.*

"Are you familiar with that part of town?" *Ivy wondered.*

"Most definitely," *Justin told her.* "I used to go to the barber shop down that way."

He was talking about the corner of Clark Street. That was, until gentrification took place in the very area he grew up.

"Hey, I know a great Dominican barber shop down the way that can get you straight," *Ivy said.*

"Oh, you do?" *he asked.*

"Yes. I'm batting 100 so far. Trust me," *she said.*

Justin nodded. "You're right. Okay, I need to go tomorrow," *he said.*

"Okay," *Ivy chirped with a bright smile.* 'Tomorrow it is!"

Justin smiled, and they sat in uncomfortable silence for a while before he asked, "Ivy, why is it that you're single?"

"That would have to be because I am so invested in running my business and attending to everyone else's happiness that I forget about myself," she said bitterly. Then she pushed the attention back on him. "And you?"

"Well...." he said, hesitating, his mind flashing back to the time he had caught his girlfriend cheating on him.

Beep! Beep! The GPS sounded, alerting them to their arrival, and Justin sighed in relief.

"To be continued," Ivy said. "This is me. On the right."

He pulled over and got out to open the door for Ivy. "Oh, why, thank you. That was nice of you!" she exclaimed.

"Oh! You're welcome, but I had to. I can't get the damn child lock off," he said, and they both laughed as they walked to Ivy's front door. Justin stopped at the entrance and turned to her. "When will I see you again?"

"Wednesday," Ivy said.

"That's in two days," he commented.

"Well, to be exact, on Mondays, Wednesdays, and Fridays at 9 am for the next three months."

Justin looked perplexed.

"I signed up for three sessions a week with you to train," Ivy pointed out.

"That's not what I meant, but that's great! I think I can tame your body. I mean, train your body," Justin elaborated.

She giggled. "See you then!"

"No, actually, I'll see you tomorrow. The barbershop, you remember?" She asked

"Yes, Until then," he said quickly, regaining his composure and watching her walk inside.

She closed the door behind her, and Justin walked back to his car. He drove off into the night, looking through radio stations for the perfect Latin song to express his feelings.

In frustration, he kept switching through stations till he found a slow and passionate bachata song. He tried his best to sing along. His tone was very-off key, but his passion and animated hand gestures made up for it.

***

Ivy walked into the room from the bathroom, having taken a warm shower, and tripped on the carpet, falling face first, her legs sore and heavy after her workout. She pulled herself up into her bed and wrapped herself under the covers. When she reached over to turn off the lights, her eyes fell on Justin's business card, and a smile crept up to her lips, but not before the pain set in from the day's workout, and she groaned in pain.

"Ugh! I'm so sore!" she yelled as she turned off the light.

On the other hand, Justin was facing a very different dilemma.

As soon as he got ready for bed, the doorbell rang, and he opened the door only to find Tiffany, his old fling, waiting outside. He stared at her for a while, hesitating when Ivy's bright smile flashed through his head. Then he opened the door wider and let her in, his fear of commitment winning over him.

Chapter 6: The Date

"Justin, there's a lot to digest here," the therapist said, taking off his glasses and looking at him.

"Shoot," Justin said casually.

"You had a great time with Ivy. Correct?" the therapist asked.

"Yes," Justin said honestly.

"So why in the world did you end the night making out with another woman?"

"Clearly, I didn't make the right decision. As they say, I was thinking with the wrong head. I told you I was insensitive toward the feelings of the women I dated," Justin clarified.

The therapist looked like he had a hard time wrapping his head around things.

"But you had a great time with Ivy, and it sounded like you guys had great chemistry."

"I did. We did. Ivy is a great girl, but regrettably, I was thinking about myself at that moment," Justin said.

His therapist sighed and said, "I hope it doesn't come back to bite you."

"Well, I am here for a reason," Justin confessed, sitting back and continuing his story.

Workout music played through the gym as Miguel walked inside toward Ron's office.

"You're late," Ron snapped as soon as he barged through the door.

"It's 8 am. I'm right on time," he insisted.

"On time is late, and being late is something I do not appreciate or tolerate or exfoliate," Ron insisted. Miguel raised his eyebrows, completely confused.

"I should have a carbohydrate..." Ron muttered to himself before shouting. "Get out there. Your 8 am is waiting."

Miguel shook his head before leaving the office. Ron saw the stash of candy on his desk and tried to fight the urge to eat it. He jumped up from behind his desk to walk away from the candy just as his eyes fell onto another hidden stash. Sadly, this time, he gave in and began to eat them.

"I can't be doing this to myself," he mumbled between chews. "I'm a damn gym owner."

Natalia walked into Ron's office without knocking, and he fumbled to hide his sweets.

"You're taking over for the rest of the day. I have lots to do!" he commanded, standing up and walking

Natalia toward the door. She held out a hand to stop him.

"Wait?! Why me?" she demanded.

"I can't let that fool, Miguel, be in charge," Ron mumbled, and they both looked outside, only to see Miguel training a client in an extremely unorthodox manner.

He was almost as bad as Justin sometimes, except Justin was actually good at his job.

At that very moment, Justin walked up to Ivy's office building and looked around before entering it. Ivy smiled when she saw him and said, "I'll be right with you."

Justin looked around, making mental notes of everything he saw. Ivy came out from the back, and together, they headed to the barbershop.

It wasn't very far, so they decided to walk. When they arrived, Justin immediately liked the look of the place. The feel was energetic and vibrant, with guys laughing and telling jokes. As soon as Justin and Ivy walked into the barbershop, they were greeted by the barbers.

"Hola!" one of the patrons said.

"Come in, my friend. How can I help you?" a barber asked, leading Justin to a chair.

"I would like a fade on the sides and short on the top," Justin told him.

"Okay, my friend. I gotchu. Come have a seat," the barber said, having Justin sit in the chair. He draped a collar and a cape over his shoulders and then grabbed his scissors, sectioning his hair before using the clippers on Justin's head.

The TV was showing a college football game featuring Cincinnati vs. Navy.

"That local boy, Trey, is nice!" one of the other barbers commented. "I have to say, he might be the nicest running back to come out of Ohio.

The barber cutting Justin's hair said, "He nice, but don't get crazy. That boy, Carlos Snow was nice."

"Facts, but... How about Maurice Clarett... Now he was damn good," the second barber said, and the entire shop seemed to agree in unison.

"All I gotta say is 2x Heisman winner Archie Griffin," A third barber insisted and the patrons in the shop all agreed once more.

"Not from Ohio, but how about that kid Mike Hart of Michigan?!" A waiting customer asked, causing all the barbers to stop cutting hair, then turn to look at each other, then the customer.

"Booo!" They yelled, then they all threw their towels at him, and everyone began to laugh. "OH, !!

IO, !! OH, !! IO," they chanted as they continued cutting hair.

"I have a question for you," Justin asked the guy cutting his hair. "Is it normal for a Latino to be affectionate? And so damn caring? I'm asking because I'm not used to someone greeting me with hugs and kisses and genuinely wanting to know about my day."

"Yes, it's our culture. My people are very passionate," the barber said.

"I can't lie. It's taking a lot to get used to. I'm not saying I want someone to treat me badly. But having someone with such a great soul is something I'm not accustomed to. It's an adjustment," Justin confessed.

"Listen, my brother," the barber said. "If you don't know what to do with her love, there will be a time when someone else comes along who does. Will you know what to do with that, then?"

Justin and the barber both glanced at Ivy who was sitting some distance away, looking through her phone.

"Make sure you are mentally and emotionally connected to her. That is if you're serious about her," the barber continued, and Justin, who was still staring at Ivy, made a mental note of what he was hearing. The barber finished the cut and passed the mirror to Justin, who stared in awe at how handsome he looked.

"Thanks, fam!" he exclaimed. "How much?"

"$20," the barber said, and Justin handed him $40.

"Okay, here's $20 for the cut and $20 for the advice," he said.

"Thank you, my friend. You got this!" the barber encouraged and dabbed him. "Come back anytime!"

"Thank you. I will," Justin promised as he and Ivy exited the shop.

"Adios, Gracias!" the barbers called out, with Justin and Ivy doing the same.

Justin opened the door for Ivy before getting into his car.

"Thank you for bringing me here today," he said. "It was really cool. It felt just like a black barber shop, with everyone talking shit."

They both laughed, and Ivy said, "I knew you would like it. You're welcome."

"You seem very attuned to your culture. Who kept you tapped in?" Justin asked.

"My Abuela," Ivy told him. "She kept a strong presence of culture in our household. It's how we all grew up at home."

"That's pretty cool," Justin murmured. "I wish I had a deeper connection to my culture."

His phone rang, and he glanced at the caller ID to see it was his mother. He ignored the call.

"Sorry about that. Continue."

Ivy noticed that he looked distraught and concerned. She reached over and placed her hand on his knee.

"My grandmother was the rock in our family," she told him. "We would sit for hours, and she would share stories with us about her upbringing, passing down stories from generations before her. You know, Justin, black and brown people have a lot in common when it comes to adversities. We go through the same racial inequalities, microaggressions, and yes, even barber shops."

They both laughed.

"Even fashion and music. I already told you I was a 2Pac fan."

"Facts," Justin said. It seems we do have a lot in common, but I call suspect on one of those.

"Oh, yeah? Which one?" Ivy challenged.

"Your music swag," he said, and Ivy chuckled. Justin put on some old-school song called *Children's Story* by Slick Rick.

"What do you know about this?" he asked.

"*Come on now, don't play me! This is my jam!*" Ivy exclaimed.

They both laughed and started singing along, enjoying the music.

"*Let's go have some fun!*" Justin cheered, and Ivy nodded.

Eventually, they stopped for some food and found themselves at LaRosa's pizzeria, eating a slice of pizza as they walked around the fountain square. Then Justin showed Ivy how to eat a cheese Coney from Skyline Chili while they rode around the streets of downtown Cincinnati by horse and buggy.

After that, he took her to the last spot on the date, a convenience store, to experience Grippo's potato chips a Cincinnati favorite. They walked and talked as she ate the chips.

"*These are great,*" she said. "*This is what a barbeque chip should taste like!*"

"*Not too hot for you?*" he asked.

"*You kidding me?*" she demanded. "*These are perfect!*"

"*When I was a kid, the flavor wasn't always consistent throughout the bag. I'd go into the store and open every bag until I found a good batch,*" Justin said. She raised an eyebrow, and he grinned. "*Don't judge me.*"

"That's awful!" she exclaimed. "But I see why. These are damn good chips!"

She ate another one as they walked along the riverbank of Cincinnati overlooking the River into Kentucky.

"I'm glad we are walking now after all we ate today. I could probably lose my license after eating all that, but it was well worth it," Ivy said.

"I haven't eaten like that since I was a kid," Justin said, making her laugh.

"So, you never answered my question the other night. Tell me why you're single. Have you ever been in love?" Ivy asked.

"I'm an Aries. I'm stubborn," Justin said, trying to divert the topic.

Ivy laughed, but then she said, "No, seriously. Answer me."

"To your first question, the answer is I'm too judgmental. To the second question, no. I haven't allowed myself to find the right person to experience love," Justin said.

"That's too bad, but knowing is half the battle. What are you doing to overcome that? Accepting love, that is?" Ivy wondered.

'I haven't done anything or care to, but I can't tell her that,' Justin thought to himself.

"Well, I'm open to the possibility," he said, and Ivy smiled.

When they arrived at Ivy's place, she invited him in. Ivy lit a few candles and turned on some music that played softly in the background. Justin looked around as she poured two glasses of wine and set them on the table.

"I'm really diggin' the music," Justin stated. "Who is it?"

"The Gypsy Kings. It's one of my favorite groups," Ivy said.

"Love it" Justin responded. "You know, I came across a style of dance called bachata, and it was really sexy. Could you please show me how to dance to it?" Justin asked.

Ivy nodded enthusiastically. "Yes! I told you I love to dance."

"You sure you don't mind?" he asked, hesitating.

"Of course not!" she exclaimed. "I would love to."

She changed the music to a different song and reached for his hand, grabbing his hips to show him the rhythm. Justin pretended to know nothing about the dance, enjoying how she led him and feigning clumsiness.

"We will keep it basic and easy for your first time. I want you to put your hand on my hip and hold my other hand with your free hand. We will step to the right three times and lightly lift your hip on three. Let's give that a try," Ivy instructed.

She counted to the beat of the music, and they began to dance the first part together, with Justin following her lead, acting as if he completely lacked confidence.

"Try to look at me and not your feet," Ivy said with a gentle smile.

"Okay, okay. I gotchu," Justin laughed.

"Ok, let's work on the other side, and then we will add a simple turn," Ivy said.

"Alright. I'm ready," Justin said, still pretending to be nervous. "Let's do this."

Ivy continued to count, and then, after a bit, she introduced another turn into the practice.

"Okay, you seemed to have mastered this very quickly! Now let's add the turn," she said. "You keep doing the same steps as we practiced, and I will begin the turn."

"Okay, let's do this!" Justin cheered, following her lead and not letting on that he had been practicing for this very moment.

They began to dance, and just as Ivy turned, Justin held her in mid-turn and brought her really close to his body while they continued to sway side to side. He then maneuvered them into a turn, bringing them face to face.

They both looked into each other's eyes, and Ivy leaned in for a kiss. Justin quickly took over the dance and turned Ivy so fast that the candles blew out. They were thrust into darkness just as their lips met, and the two shared their first kiss.

The next morning, while at the gym, the thought of last night's kiss crossed Justin's mind as he trained his client.

When the session ended, they walked over to Justin's office to go over the client's goals and nutrition plans.

"So, how is everything going with the nutritional plan?" Justin asked.

"It's going great!" Mr. Evans, his client, said. "I'm doing everything you told me. Training with weights five times a week, cardio daily, five small meals a day, eating every three hours, high protein, low carbohydrates, and lots of veggies. All just like you said."

Justin smiled in encouragement and exclaimed, "Okay, awesome!"

"It was a struggle at first, but it is getting better," Mr. Evans admitted.

"You're doing everything?" Justin asked, and Mr. Evans smiled, nodding emphatically.

"Yes!" he declared.

"It's been a month. Let's see where we are," Justin said, directing Mr. Evans to step onto the body scanner.

"I always feel like I need to hold in my stomach when I get on these things," his client complained and tried to suck in his stomach, but it was so big that his efforts went unnoticed.

Justin looked at the body scanner and noticed Mr. Evans had only lost 10 lbs.

"Well, according to the scanner, you lost ten pounds. I'd like you to stay focused on everything. I know it's rough but I promise the outcome will be worth it," Justin said.

Mr. Evans nodded, and Justin continued, "Okay, Mr. Evans, you're making gains. But I want you to give this form to your physician so he can evaluate you and then return it to me. There is nothing to be concerned with; it's just so I can be better at my job, and you can be your best self."

"Thank you, Justin. Thank you for being my trainer. I know I haven't lost a lot of weight compared to your other clients, but it's more than what I've lost *in the last two years, and it's all because of you,"* Mr. Evans said, making Justin smile, and shake his head.

"No, this is your journey. I'm just here to guide you. You have to do the work, and you have," Justin insisted as they exited out of the office. Then he walked over to Ron, who was on the stair climber, drench in sweat going extra hard.

"Boss, can I talk to you?" he asked.

"Sure, come to my office," Ron said, eager to stop exercising. He rushed to his office and popped an M&M into his mouth, swallowing quickly and fake coughing just as Justin entered the office.

"These damn allergies!" Ron said dramatically as Justin sat in the chair in front of the desk.

Justin rolled his eyes, knowing full well what Ron had done, and said, "Anyway, boss. You know I'm seeing Ivy, and I like her. She's not like the other girls. She's truly different. I feel comfortable being myself when I'm with her. My dilemma is I just don't know how to open up to her. Do you have any suggestions?"

Ron held up an M&M and talked slowly, savoring the M&M, "Being vulnerable is a tough subject for a fella. Take this M&M, for example. It has an exterior coating that shelters all of its chocolaty goodness inside of it. And once you commit to it, it lets down its barriers to show all the goodness inside it has to offer. Do you understand, son?"

Justin nodded, suppressing a grimace, and said, "Oddly enough, I think I do. Thank you."

"No problem, son," Ron said graciously. "Now, shut the door behind you. I have tons of paperwork to attend to." He continued to stare at the M&M in his hand as if just thinking about it.

"Yes sir, thanks again," Justin said, and Ron gestured for him to leave so that he could actually eat the M&M, too impatient to wait any longer.

Justin exited Ron's office and took a glanced around and saw that Natalia was busy training a client and close by was Natalia's girlfriend, Jane, watching every rep.

From the other side, Miguel was fast approaching him.

"Yo, where have you been? I haven't heard from or seen you in days," Miguel said.

"Me and Ivy had been kicking it these past few days. Dude, she wiped food off my face with her finger. No one has ever done that," Justin said, awe-filling his tone.

"Sound's great," Miguel said before brushing it away. "Now, let me tell you my good news."

"What's up?" Justin asked.

"I was here yesterday, doing me when this little shawty came in looking to join. She was bad. You already know she had a fatty on her," Miguel explained.

"Okay, did you get her number?" Justin asked.

"No doubt," Miguel said with a wink, and Justin grinned.

"Okay, check it. See if she wants to come out tonight. Ivy and I are hitting this new spot tonight. y'all meet us there?" Justin said.

Miguel nodded in agreement. "Done. Hit me up with the info later on," he said.

"Alright, I'm out," Justin declared, walking toward the gym exit.

Chapter 7: The Club

"What was different about Ivy from all the other women you dated?" The therapist asked once Justin paused to take a breath.

"From day one, I felt that she was genuine. And I could trust her with my feelings," Justin explained.

The therapist smiled and gestured for him to continue, which he promptly did.

Justin and Ivy sat at the table across from Miguel, both of them dressed up for the occasion and slightly impatient.

"Miguel, where is she? It's been 45 minutes?" Justin asked, his tone annoyed.

"She should be walking in shortly. She just pulled in," Miguel replied, glancing down at his phone.

"Jay said you met her at the gym. Have you guys gotten to know each other?" Ivy gently asked, making polite small talk.

"Yeah," Miguel said, a soft smile creeping up on his lips. "She's single, which is hard to believe. No kids. She seems really down to earth and has a body that don't stop. Just how I like it." Ivy laughed.

Miguel's date, Keisha, walked in through the door.

"She's here," Miquel said. He had been looking at the entrance.

Justin turned to look. "You said she has a body that don't quit, right?"

"Yes sirrrr!" Miguel said as Justin looked over to where Miguel had indicated.

"Yes, that's her," he said. *"Short body caddy."*

"My guy, that's not a caddy. That's a big body escalade," Justin corrected, trying to hold back a smirk, and Ivy hit Justin on the arm.

"HE SAID IT! I'M JUST SAYING THAT SHE AIN'T NO CADDY! MORE LIKE A SUBURBAN!" Justin exclaimed, trying to defend himself while Ivy glared at him.

"Stop it!" Ivy snapped, smiling at how adorable she was.

"Be quiet, stupid," Miguel said, shushing him just before Keisha walked toward them. He stood up and hugged her. Then Ivy introduced herself with a smile and a hug, and Justin shook her hand.

"You look amazing. Glad you came out," Miguel said, glancing at her sparkly dress.

"I was surprised that you called," Keisha admitted. *"Thanks for inviting me."*

"Your hair looks great. Where do you go?" Ivy asked her.

Keisha smiled. "I did it myself," she said.

"Yeah? It looks great!" Miguel commented, and Ivy nodded.

"I haven't found a good hairdresser since I moved here. I may have to start coming to you, girl!" Ivy said, and Keisha smiled.

"Of course!" she said.

"Miguel says you guys had a great workout. How do you think it went?" Justin asked Keisha, who blushed and exchanged a shy smile with Miguel.

"It went well. I'm a little sore," she told them.

"That's normal," Justin said, nodding. "Just listen to your trainer. He won't steer you wrong."

Ivy agreed, and Miguel smiled in appreciation. A new song came on, and Ivy immediately perked up.

"I love this song! Keisha, you wanna come and dance with me?" she asked.

Keisha was hesitant, but Ivy went off to the dance floor and started dancing. She looked back at the table and gestured for Keisha to join her, trying to make her feel more comfortable. Keisha was still unsure. She looked around the club before pulling her hair up in a bun and walking to the dance floor. However, the music loosened her up, and soon, she kicked her shoes off and started dancing. Miguel looked over at her and felt like it was all happening in slow motion. He was completely enraptured by her.

"Keisha is getting it!" Justin cheered.

"Yes, she is," Miguel agreed. "Does Ivy dance professionally?"

Justin nodded, his eyes glued to Ivy, unmoving, "No, she said it's just a hobby, but she's damn good at it. She has me at full attention, my dude."

He was mesmerized by every single thing about her, unable to wrench his eyes away.

The song ended, and both women walked to the restroom to fix their clothes, making small talk as they did so. They fixed their makeup and sprayed more perfume before going back outside.

"You're a badass on the dance floor," Ivy commented appreciatively.

"I had fun. Thank you," Keisha said. "Can I ask you a question?"

"Yes, of course," Ivy replied curiously.

"You, Justin, and Miguel look great. It's not hard to see that I'm not in the best shape," she started, fiddling with her finger nervously.

Ivy's eyes widened, and she said, "You're beautiful."

It was true, and nothing could change her opinion.

"Yeah, for a big girl," Keisha murmured. "I don't know what Miguel sees in me."

"Keisha! No, you-" Ivy started to say but was cut off.

"It's okay. It's true. Can you help me with my nutrition? Miguel says that you are a nutritionist," Keisha said. Ivy smiled faintly and nodded.

"Yes," she said.

"And one more thing," Keisha said, hesitating. Her voice dropped to a whisper. "Can you keep this between us?"

"I would be glad to help you," Ivy said. "It's not a problem."

Keisha grinned, all her pearly white teeth flashing in the dull lights, making her look even more beautiful. "Thank you, girl!" she exclaimed.

"Let's get together next week?" Ivy suggested. "Let me know when you have time."

Justin and Miguel sat at the table and talked while they waited for the girls.

"You know man, Ivy is a good girl. I just don't know if I want to settle down with her or continue to be a single man," Justin said.

"What's the issue?" Miguel questioned, slightly confused about Justin's dilemma. "If you are feeling her, make it happen. I know the guys clowned you in high school for telling Amber you love her. And it did turn out to be a mistake since she was in the closet with that huge kid getting her freak on. But that was over ten years ago. A lot has changed since then. We grown."

"You know what?" Justin asked all of a sudden. "I just realized, at this very moment, that I have never told anyone outside of Amber that I love them. I guess I blocked it all out after that night. I'm 27 years old and have never told my family I love them."

Justin looked at Miguel and thought, 'I've never even told my best friend I love him.'

Miguel carried on with the conversation and said, "Are you still ignoring your mom's calls?"

"Yes," Justin said shortly, wanting to avoid the topic entirely.

"I know how you feel about her, but you better address your childhood traumas; otherwise, your future relationships will suffer," his best friend told him.

Justin sighed and said, "I just don't know if I'm willing to share me with someone else right now. I like going on dates and meeting new people. And I like having my Saturdays, to myself, just watching football drama free. And what I hate especially is PDA, look at that couple over there, for example, with the matching outfits, it's all corny. I can't do it.

He glared at the couples wearing matching outfits and making out in public, grimacing slightly.

"It's ok to be goofy and corny with your girl, Jay. That's your girl. You got her already. No need to continue to hide behind a fake persona," Miguel explained, and Justin listened intently, trying to process it.

"Jay, you can lie to me, but be honest with yourself. Deep down inside, you wanna turn your playa' card in. Why else would you still be TV surfing at night to watch 'The Cosby Show' or 'My Wife and Kids'?" Miguel demanded. He placed his hands on Justin's shoulder and smiled encouragingly. "No more TV, it's time to experience love firsthand."

The girls walked out of the bathroom, and the guys stopped talking, watching as their dates made their way toward them.

Chapter 8: Maternal Affection

The therapist leaned forward in his chair, holding out his hands. "Okay. Stop there, please!"

Justin sat up from the couch he was lying down on and looked up at him in question.

"Tell me," his therapist said. "What was Miguel alluding to when he said, "There's a reason you watch those particular shows? What were you looking for?"

Justin hesitated. "I know it's only TV, but I watch those two particular shows because they gave me insight into what a loving relationship looks like. I got to see how they interacted with each other, how both men were silly and corny with their partner, and how loving they were and still manly."

"Interesting," the therapist commented, raising a brow. "So, you watch these two men as your model examples of how you should treat your partner? Did it help you in your relationships?

"Yes, and no. It's all I had as a positive example. I say no because while I definitely understood what I needed to improve, I still have a hard time following through," Justin admitted.

"Got it! Don't you have any friends or family members who are happily married? How about your own parents?" the therapist wondered.

Justin looked away, trying to hide his pain before saying, "Dad passed away when I was really young, so I don't remember anything about my parent's marriage. No one in my family or friends' parents were married when I was coming up." He paused. "There was no one."

"Justin, who do you talk to when you're upset? Or when you just wanna express what's on your mind?" his therapist probed.

"No one," Justin said. "I keep everything to myself."

"That's not good for your mental health or well-being," his therapist pointed out.

"I don't feel comfortable opening up to anyone, especially another man," Justin added as an afterthought.

"We as men, particularly men of color, need to get over the stigma of asking for help and talking to other men. It's the only way we're going to help each other and heal ourselves. Please carry on with your story," the therapist instructed, and Justin nodded.

He laid back down on the sofa and began to speak. "Where did I leave off at? Okay, yes. We left the club early."

Ivy and Justin walked through the door of Justin's place, and he closed the door behind her.

"I had a great time. And Keisha really cut loose, didn't she?" Ivy asked with a fond smile.

"Yes," Justin said. "For someone who seems to be very shy, she didn't hold back."

Ivy grinned and said, "I like her."

"I think Miguel does too," Justin mused, turning on the lights.

"Okay, baby. I'm about to lay it down. I'm tired, okay?" Ivy murmured.

Justin turned to her and said, "I'm going to stay up for a little to watch TV."

"Okay, don't be too long," Ivy told him just as Justin plopped himself down on the couch. She kissed him before entering the bedroom, and Justin turned on the TV, surfing through the channels to find something interesting.

Finally, he landed on a favorite. 'My Wife and Kids' where he watched to study the married couple behavior. He noticed how they interacted and how it was okay to be silly with the people you cared about, just like Miguel had said. He reflected on his conversation with Miguel, and soon, his thoughts drifted to his mom.

Meanwhile, Miguel sat on the couch in Keisha's living room, waiting for her. When she exited the bedroom wearing a see-through outfit, a mask, holding a whip, his mouth dropped open in slight surprise.

"I thought you were shy?!" Miguel exclaimed as she walked toward him.

Keisha smiled seductively. "Every shy girl has a wild side," she whispered before striking him with a whip.

***

The next morning Justin found himself staring at the door of his mom's house, hesitating. Finally, he walked up to the door and rang the bell, waiting till she answered.

"Hello, mom," he said when he saw her.

"You haven't been answering my phone calls. I was starting to think you were adult-napped," his mom complained.

"No," Justin said with a slight sigh. "Just busy."

"Okay. So, what brings you by? Finally!" she said, beckoning him inside and ushering him toward the couch.

He took a seat and said, "I'm here because I'm kinda seeing someone, and I'm having a hard time opening up to her," he told her.

"Okay...." his mom said, looking confused, wondering why he was talking to her about his love life.

Justin hesitated and then finally decided to let everything out. "Well, mom," he started. *"It's because of you. I feel awkward when I hug her. That's because I felt your awkwardness when you hugged me. It's because of you that I'm not affectionate. You weren't affectionate toward me, and because of you, it's hard for me to open up to anyone. And because of that upbringing, there's a detachment with anyone I'm dating; it feels normal to keep moving on to the next girl rather than trying to make it work with that one individual."*

His mom grimaced, looking like she was going to say something, but Justin cut her off.

"You know, it's easy for me to pretend with each girl initially. Holding hands, kissing, and showing how affectionate I am. However, the longer I keep up with the lie, my skin crawls with every kiss and hug. Something as simple as holding hands is torture. And, when I'm shown love, I don't know how to receive it or reciprocate it. I go blank. I didn't know why at first, but internally I knew it was because of you," he ranted.

"Don't blame your relationship issues on me," his mom said angrily. *"I was always there for you. I*

bought you whatever you asked for. I bought you your first car. And your first-"

"Being there for me financially isn't the same as being emotionally invested in me, mom," Justin argued. "What's my favorite color? What's my favorite food? My likes and dislikes? You don't know anything about me. You've never even hugged me or complimented me."

"That's not true!" his mom snapped.

Justin shook his head. "Think about it. You know it's true," he muttered. He stood up and started to leave.

"You're grown now," his mom said abruptly, stopping him in his tracks. "Why tell me now? There's nothing I can do about it now!"

Justin turned to look at her and said, "This is the first girl I have really liked. I'm just trying to make things right in my past so I have a fair chance at a future with her."

"I do love you," his mom told him.

"Ditto, mom...ditto," he replied, leaving the house and closing the door behind him.

Chapter 9: Unable to Say the Words

The sun shone brightly through the therapist's window, and he squinted to look at Justin.

"So, Justin, how did it feel to speak with your mother?" he asked.

"It felt great. I had a lot of built-up anger I was holding on to, and it made me resent her, making it hard to communicate with her," he confessed.

"Good for you," the therapist said. "I'm glad you were finally able to express yourself. That was huge, and I'll tell you why."

Justin sat up, listening closely as his therapist continued.

"You're a guy having vulnerability problems, and at the same time, you're trying to figure out all these newfound emotions. Am I right?"

"YES!" Justin exclaimed, feeling glad about being understood.

"Justin, love is a form of intimacy and you can't have intimacy without vulnerability. If your past makes you avoid vulnerability, you'll never have intimacy. I know being guarded feels like self-defense, but in the long term, it's self-harm," the therapist told him. "Does that make sense?"

"Yes," Justin said with a nod, agreeing fully.

"You have another thing to think about, and I don't know if it ever crossed your mind, but your mother is simply reflecting on how she was raised," the therapist said.

Justin furrowed his brows, confused.

"In other words," his therapist continued, "What you're experiencing is exactly what your mother, your grandmother, and her mother before her, did. So, you can either correct it now or continue to pass this down to your kids and so forth."

Justin remained silent, taking his time to think about it. The therapist waited for Justin, letting the thought sink in.

"Please continue," the therapist finally said, and Justin nodded.

Ivy was assisting a client when Justin walked in.

"I'll be right with you," she told him, and he nodded.

"No problem. Take your time," he said with a soft smile, watching her.

Ivy smiled gratefully and turned back to her client.

"Make sure you're prepping your food ahead of time and stay consistent. Also, I want you to stay off

the scale and away from the mirror to prevent you from judging yourself. You're only tearing yourself down," she instructed.

"You're right," the client said. "I have to do better with that."

Justin walked around, checking out Ivy's place, and saw a picture of Ivy and her mother. He could feel the love between her and her mother, smiling joyfully as he held the picture to look at it closely.

"Ma'am, if I may?" Justin said, looking at the client, having overheard the conversation between her and Ivy.

"I'm all ears!" the client said.

"Ivy is absolutely right about that mirror. The mirror is not your friend. I want you only in front of the mirror when you are dressed. That means when you're getting out of the shower, do not look until you are dressed. I'm sure you're asking yourself why? And I'll tell you why. See, looking in the mirror will make you depressed, and then you're more likely to go back to making bad choices because you're looking for instant gratification, and when you don't see that, you slowly lose motivation," Justin explained.

He sat in the chair next to Ivy's client, and Ivy nodded reassuringly.

"When you're on a diet, you want to see instant results, and that's normal, But we must be honest with ourselves on what the expectations are and be patient about seeing results.

"This takes time, so what I want you to do is mark your calendar 16 weeks out from today. In 16 weeks, when you step back on that scale, you're going to see results. And you know why? Because in the next 16 weeks, you're going to work your butt off to see those results you were looking for in the first week," Justin continued, and Ivy smiled.

"Okay. That makes sense. I'm going to do it!" the client exclaimed.

"Are you married?" Justin wondered.

"Yes, I am," she said, and Justin nodded.

"Let me show you some exercises you can do with your husband," he said, showing the client some resistance training exercises that impressed Ivy.

"Oh my! That was great. I've never felt like this after working out. I feel amazing! You know, you guys should go into business together," the client encouraged, making Justin and Ivy glance at each other with a smile.

"Thank you for the help," the client continued. "May I set my appointments up for the next coming weeks? I plan to stay motivated."

"Of course. I can't wait to see your progress! Good luck!" Ivy told her. The client walked to Justin and shook his hand, thanking him.

Then Ivy and Justin turned to look at her as she left.

"What do you think?" Ivy finally asked.

"About what?" Justin wondered.

"About what she said. Us. Going into business together?" she murmured.

Justin shrugged, feeling slightly uncomfortable with the thought of it.

"It's not a bad look. Let's talk about it later?" he said shortly. *"I need to get to the gym."*

"Okay," Ivy said, hesitating. *"I'll see you later."*

The gym had been Justin's safe haven over the years; it was his go-to to sort out everything.

'Nothing like an early morning session to get the blood going,' Justin thought.

Justin was no slouch in the gym; that's why he was well-revered and known as the best trainer in the area. And that morning, if anyone watched, they would see why.

He attacked the treadmill like a racecar on a racetrack, not slowing down one second at top speed for 45 min, but he was just getting started. The next victims: the battle rope and slam balls, where he let's go the most built-up energy with each crushing slam.

He destroyed it and followed it up with burpees, exploding from the floor to the ceiling with every lift-off while drenched in sweat and breathing heavily, but feeling refreshed and having found some clarity from the workout.

After the workout, Justin hit the shower and got dressed quickly.

Miquel walked into the locker room. "I see you got it in already."

"Yeah. I had some things to sort out with my mom and Ivy in my head. I took your advice and went to go see mom," Justin said.

"Oh yeah?" Miguel asked. "How did that go?"

"Typical mom denial, but you know what? I'm glad I went and got that off my chest," he said.

"I'm gonna give Ivy a real chance. No more other girls. And I'm going to be more open to being vulnerable," Justin said.

"What about holding hands and kissing in public?" Miguel teased.

"I'm open to that, I guess," Justin said, not sounding too confident.

"And matching outfits?" Miguel jokingly asked, and Justin made a choking sound.

"Nah. That, I...can't do," Justin said.

"I'm proud of you bro!" Miguel said.

"Thank you, man. Tell me about you and Keisha," Justin said, changing the topic.

"Yo, after we left the club, shorty went from The Preacher's Daughter to Devil's Advocate!" Miguel said. "She went in on me. Our training sessions have been pretty intense, and the sex has been crazy."

"Great on the sessions, but Devil's Advocate?... that's scary," Justin replied.

"Yes," Miguel said with a nod, looking frightened. "Things got wild."

***

Justin arrived at Ivy's front door and knocked on the door.

"I'm glad you decided to come over for dinner," Ivy said, opening the door and letting him in. She pulled him into a hug and laid a gentle kiss on his lips.

"Thanks for asking me over," Justin said.

Ivy grinned and playfully pinched his cheek.

"Go wash your hands in the restroom," she instructed.

Justin smiled and headed over to the bathroom.

He paused to look at a picture frame on the wall with the words:

"Make every moment count, take the time to reflect on what truly matters to you, and let your heart be your guide. Pursue your dreams and goals, and make the most of every moment. With determination and positivity, you can make your life amazing."

- Love, Mom.

Justin quickly washed his hands and returned to Ivy, who was preparing the dishes. He sneaked up behind her, pulling her into a hug and kissing her cheek.

Ivy giggled, turning her head toward him.

"What brought that on?" she wondered.

"Oh, I just wanted to thank you for being you," Justin said honestly.

Ivy smiled softly. "Thank you for allowing me to be me."

Justin sat down at the table, and Ivy shook her head.

"We're not sitting at the table. We're out here," she said. "Follow me."

She took him out on the patio, decorated beautifully with culturally significant objects. It was mainly set up in a black, brown, and beige theme, with lit candles, making the ambiance cozy and inviting.

"Wow, this is really nice!" Justin said, looking around. It had started to rain, and they could see it fall while they snuggled up cozily.

"Thank you," Ivy said, sounding pleased. "I'm glad you liked it."

"This is great, and the food looks amazing!" Justin complimented. He sat down and waited for her to do the same.

"It's called arroz con pollo," she said once she had taken her seat. "Rice and chicken."

"It looks great!" Justin said. His phone rang, and he glanced at the caller ID to see it was his mother. He ignored the call, and Ivy's lips twisted into a curious pout.

"Can I ask you a question?" she wondered.

"Of course," he said,

She hesitated slightly before saying, "Why don't you answer the phone when your mother calls?"

Justin paused. "If you had asked me this question a week ago, I don't know what I would have told you. Now... the answer is she's the source of many of my childhood memories I would like to forget. And, unintentionally, she's the reason why I approach relationships as I do," he explained, knowing he was treading dangerous waters.

"How so?" she asked.

"My mother and I don't have a loving relationship. No affection ever, and because of that, I express myself the same way in my relationships. I feel awkward when showing a vulnerable side of myself," Justin admitted.

"I'm so sorry this happened to you," Ivy said. "But just maybe, I'm guessing she was brought up the same way, and she's reflecting that on you. It's a generational curse, and you were strong enough to break away from it. That's a big deal."

Justin paused, taking in her comforting words.

"I guess so," he said shortly.

"Why'd you say that?" she asked.

"Yes, I was able to acknowledge it," Justin admitted. "Maybe I was even strong enough to start doing something about it, but it's still a struggle every day I'm with you. I wanna hug you and kiss you, but there's a hold on me, and it's hard. It's hard to open up. I think about you all day, how I miss you, all the things I wanna do to you... But then I see you, and I freeze."

Ivy got up from the dinner table and took Justin's hands, pulling him closer and holding him.

"I'm here for you," she said. "I'm here to help."

She looked into Justin's eyes while he tried to swallow against the lump in his throat, focusing on the soft pitter-patter of the rain.

"I will not hurt you," she continued. "I love you."

Justin paused, the words sitting at the tip of his tongue. He wanted to say it back. He really did; instead, all that he said was, "Ditto!" Ivy stepped back, understanding something was wrong, and looked at Justin with furrowed brows. His heart sank, and a feeling of extreme sorrow washed over him.

Chapter 10: A Decision to Make

"You said ditto to the woman that finally made you feel alive?" Justin's therapist asked, unable to process it.

"Yes," Justin clarified.

"You said ditto to the woman that finally made you feel alive?" his therapist repeated, stressed.

"Yes," Justin admitted with a nod. "Nothing scares me more than someone loving me one day and deciding they don't want me the next. I have to really know she loves me."

The therapist gestured for him to continue, and he did.

They had finished dinner and spent the night together, but Ivy could tell he was distant. When he woke up, her side of the bed was empty, and he could smell coffee. She knocked on the door and smiled when he looked up.

"Here you are," she said, bringing him some coffee.

"Thank you," Justin told her, unable to look her in the eye.

"What was 'ditto' about last night?" Ivy said, finally bringing it up.

"Oh, that was nothing," Justin lied, still not looking at her.

Ivy sat next to Justin and gently held his head so she could look directly into his eyes.

"You sure?" she asked.

"Yes! What's going on?" he said, looking away from her.

"Okay, never mind," she said, letting go of him when she realized he was not going to answer. *"We didn't get a chance to talk last night about what Mrs. Brown said."*

"Hey, it's not my fault someone named Ivy couldn't keep their grimy green thumbs off me," Justin said, feeling better after the joke.

"Green thumbs?" Ivy asked, a bout of laughter following the words.

"Yeah, green thumbs. Your name is Ivy, and you were all over me," he joked.

"That's not funny," Ivy said.

He could see her trying not to smile.

"I thought it was pretty funny. Anywho, I thought about working together, and I think it's a great idea," Justin said.

Ivy cheered up and exclaimed, "Yay! I'm so excited! I have the perfect name for our business!"

"Okay, what is it?" he asked.

"Justus fitness and Nutrition," Ivy said, sounding nervous.

"You know?" Justin asked, thinking about it. "I like it." He got up from the bed, placed his coffee on the dresser and got dressed quickly. "Okay. Let's do our homework. We can make it happen."

Ivy stood up and hugged him.

"Thank you!" she said.

Justin nodded.

"Okay. I'm out. I have a 9 am appointment," he explained, glancing at his watch.

"Have a great day. See you later," Ivy said, kissing him and then watching as he left the room. She settled herself on her bed, finishing the rest of her coffee.

Justin breathed a sigh of relief, glad that Ivy had not questioned him too much about the 'ditto' thing. He was still thinking about it when he walked in through the gym's door.

"Your 9 am is in your office," Natalia stated dryly as soon as she saw him.

"Okay. Thank you," he said, walking toward his office.

As soon as he opened the door, he noticed his client laying across the desk wearing nothing but lingerie. He immediately closed the door and walked away, ignoring her. He was not a completely changed man, but he needed to at least try.

The next morning, when Justin walked into the gym, he noticed one of their female members jogging on the treadmills. She flirtatiously waved at him, but he looked away, barely acknowledging her existence. Ron, who had been standing near his office, took notice of this unusual behavior and wondered what had changed.

The next morning, Justin walked into work with a smile. When he got there, Ivy was already waiting for him. They quickly finished the session, and Ivy sneaked him a kiss before leaving the gym.

Tiffany, Justin's old fling, looked at them with slight disgust and walked off.

Ron, on the other hand, smiled at the sight. "Justin! Step into my office," he called out.

"What's going on?" Justin asked, walking toward one of the chairs but not sitting down.

"I've been watching you the past few weeks, and I never thought I would be saying this, but- It's yours. The gym is yours. You're truly a different person, and I'm proud of you," Ron announced.

Justin looked confused.

"Wait, what?" he asked hesitatingly. "Thank you. I don't know how I feel now. It's all I've wanted for the past several years, but a lot has changed. The only reason why you see a change in me is because of Ivy."

"You know, Justin? A diamond is merely a lump of coal that did well under pressure. I'm sure you'll make the right decision. The offer is on the table. I'll give you time to think about it," Ron said wisely.

"Thank you," Justin mumbled, not knowing what else to say. "And thanks again for the opportunity."

He walked out of Ron's office, lost in thought, and headed to his own. Tiffany walked into his office as soon as he had settled behind his desk.

"So, I was thinking. Maybe we can do it right here. On your desk," she suggested.

Justin shook his head.

"Nah, that's not going to happen. I'm seeing someone," he said shortly.

Tiffany leaned over the desk sucking on her finger, "That's never stopped you before."

"Can you please leave?" Justin demanded irritably. "I have some work to attend to."

"Wow, okay. This is a first," she snapped, offended, and left his office. Justin sat back in his chair and shook his head in disbelief.

Once work was over and he was back in his apartment, Ron's words came back to him. He put on some music, took off his shirt, and started to jog on the treadmill, knowing it would help him clear his mind.

Chapter 11: Art and Ivy

Present Day

"So, you finally got what you wanted. The job, the girl, but... now you have to decide what to hold on to and what to let go," Justin's therapist stated, summing everything up.

Justin sat up and turned around so he could listen properly.

"Yes. That's why I'm here today. I never imagined that this would be my struggle," Justin said.

"I'm not here to point you in one direction or another. My only hope is to give you insight. Let me explain. I've listened to you speak all day. For once, stop speaking with your mouth and listen to your heart!" the therapist exclaimed.

Justin stood up and walked over to the therapist. He shook his head and smiled with sadness on his face.

"Please call me and let me know how it all works out for you," the therapist said.

Justin nodded, shook the therapist's hand, and left the office.

It was time to give love a chance again.

Justin walked into the gym and looked at his appointment sheet for the day. Anxious, he glanced out of his office window and noticed Jane closely watching Natalia while she trained a male member.

Suddenly, Justin got up from his office chair, approached Jane, and sat beside her while she continued exercising on the bike.

"I'm not really the one to be giving relationship advice, but don't you know Natalia loves you?" Justin asked, trying to make sure his tone was not rude.

"Yes," Jane said.

"Do you love her?" Justin asked.

Jane looked at him wide-eyed.

"Of course," she exclaimed.

"In a relationship, trust is just as important as love because it will enhance the love," he said, then he quickly got up and walked to his office, hoping he hadn't intruded. Miguel followed him inside, having overheard the entire thing.

Miguel closed the door and sat in the chair in front of Justin's desk.

"Are you okay, fam?" he asked.

"Well, Ron offered the LA gym to me," Justin said.

"What!? About time!" Miguel exclaimed, Congrats. "Are we happy?"

"I'm not sure. You know this is all I wanted, but then there's Ivy," Justin said with a sigh.

"I know LA is all we both wanted at one point-" Miguel started to say, but Justin cut him off.

"What do you mean at one point? If I leave, you won't come with me?" he demanded.

"Well, no," Miguel said decidedly. "I'm with Keisha now."

"You barely know her! I've known you forever!" Justin exclaimed.

"Well, Jay, I'm in love with her," Miguel told him.

"What? You love her?" Justin demanded. "Talk about being soft. I thought you would always have my back."

Miguel got up to walk out of the office. He stopped at the door and looked back.

"Well, Jay, I've always shown you much love, even more than you've ever shown me. And just like you said, you've never shown love back. But, for the first time in my life, I've found a friend who will," Miguel said softly before walking out of the office.

***

Ivy glanced at the mirror and admired her reflection.

"Thank you for doing my hair here, girl!" she said brightly, looking at Keisha.

"Really, it was no problem! After all, it's the least I can do for all your help," Keisha replied cheerfully.

"By the way, you look great! How much have you lost?" Ivy asked.

"60 pounds!" Keisha told her confidently.

"You look amazing," Ivy told her. "What does Miguel think?"

Keisha thought back to the time she was sleeping with Miguel, and he spanked her on the butt, saying, 'short body caddy'!!

"I think he likes my results," she replied.

They both broke out into a laugh and then Keisha asked, "How are things with you and Justin?"

Ivy hesitated.

"You know? Things had been going well. But last night, I told him I love him, and this fool said ditto to me," she confided.

"Ditto?" Keisha wondered.

"Yes, and then made light of it as if it was nothing!" Ivy complained. "So, I didn't push it."

"What do you think?" Keisha probed.

"I know he's been through a lot with him not having a relationship with his parents. But I don't deserve ditto! I'm not sure how I feel about it," Ivy said honestly.

"It was definitely wrong, but like you said, he's a work in progress," Keisha said.

"That is true," Ivy agreed.

"Miguel told me Justin is also holding onto being hurt by someone he thought he loved in high school," Keisha added.

"So, he lied to me when I first asked him if he had ever been in love before," Ivy asked, raising her eyebrows. She took a seat at her desk and placed her head in her hands, pinching the skin between her eyebrows.

"I'm sorry, girl. I would have told you sooner. I really didn't think it was anything," Keisha said.

Ivy looked up and smiled reassuringly.

"No worries. It's not your fault," she said.

Keisha walked over and pulled up a seat near Ivy, sitting down.

"The only reason I'm saying anything now is because you guys are magic when you are together. And I wanna see y'all win," she murmured.

"Thank you, girl," Ivy said with a weak smile.

"On the outside, looking in, I can see he loves you, especially when he talks about you. You can see it when he looks at you," Keisha continued, making Ivy smirk. "He loves you; he just doesn't know how to express it yet."

Ivy nodded dejectedly, so Keisha changed the subject, and they began to talk about something else.

Eventually, Ivy and Keisha walked out of Ivy's office, Ivy locked up behind her as Keisha walked ahead. Keisha spotted Justin waiting for Ivy at the entrance in his car and waved to him.

"Hi, Justin," she called out.

"Hey, Keisha. You look great!" he complimented.

"Thank you," Keisha said.

Justin had his head down, eyes on his phone, when Ivy walked out he glanced up. Suddenly his eyes widened when he saw Ivy with her new hairstyle. He was mesmerized and tried not to gawk while she walked toward the car.

"Your hair looks great," he said. "You look amazing."

"Thank you," Ivy replied. "What's going on? You sounded so down on the phone. I'm glad you came out. I know you didn't really want to."

"Well, you didn't give me a choice," Justin joked.

"I couldn't just let you sit in the house and sulk," Ivy told him. "And you still haven't told me what's wrong."

"Just some things I need to sort out," Justin said shortly.

"Well, you can get back to that soon enough, but for now, let's go have some fun," Ivy said, trying to restrain her disappointment with Justin not giving her insight on what was wrong.

"Where are we going?" Justin asked.

"You'll see," Ivy said.

They pulled up to an unassuming building.

"Here?" Justin asked

"Here," Ivy said with a nod. They got out of the car and walked inside.

"What is this place?"

"Body art. It's going to be fun. I didn't want to leave you at home, depressed. I also wanted to share some good news with you," Ivy chimed.

Justin and Ivy were greeted by a host and handed some paint supplies before being ushered to their seats.

The host gestured to Ivy and Justin.

"This is the Darby's, and these are the Newman's. Everybody, please welcome Ivy and Justin," she introduced warmly.

"Hi," the class said in unison, making them smile.

"Okay, have a seat, you guys," the host said. "You are just in time. We're about to begin."

"Great!" Ivy exclaimed while she and Justin took their seats.

The host brought over two glasses of wine and said, "Here you guys go."

All the couples began painting, and Justin turned to Ivy.

"What was your good news?" he asked.

"Oh yeah! I came across a building for us. For your gym and my nutritional center," Ivy clarified then paused.

Justin stopped painting and turned to her.

"And," he said.

"The only thing is we have to bid on it, and several bids are already in. Do you think we can place a bid tomorrow?" she asked.

"Hmm, Okay. Let's make a bid," Justin sighed and then nodded, turning back to his painting. Ivy, overwhelmed with excitement, held it in and continued to have a good time, drinking wine and eating the provided appetizers.

Eventually, all of them were done.

"Great job, everyone. These look great!" the host encouraged. "Now I have something else if you guys are interested. It's body art, and you're the canvas."

"What exactly does that entail?" one of the painters asked.

"Painting your backside with paint then laying down on the canvas to produce beautiful paintings like these," the host explained. She turned around and pointed to some of the paintings on display.

"Those are amazing. We're in!" one of the women called out.

"We're down, also!" another couple cheered excitedly.

"We have to!" Ivy insisted, turning to Justin.

"Okay," Justin said with a nod. "Let's do it."

"We're in!" Ivy called out to the host, a bright smile pulling at her lips.

"Great! Let's get started. Come with me," the host instructed. She led the couples to a hall with multiple rooms. "The person who's getting painted on will need an apron and nothing else. Make sure to open your legs a little wide for best results."

"You're going to see my behind," Justin whispered to Ivy.

She raised a brow. "I've already seen your behind."

They both laughed, and the host assigned each of them a room, handing out some aprons.

Ivy waited for Justin to shed his clothes and quickly painted him.

"I didn't notice your cheeks had dimples. I guess I missed that," Ivy commented.

"You like?" Justin joked.

"Yeah. It's nice!" Ivy confessed. She finished up her painting, and they switched. When Ivy had her apron on, Justin couldn't help but stare at her.

"Are you ready? What are you doing, silly?" Ivy asked.

"No, I am not ready," Justin said.

"Spread your legs some more. You heard the host."

He helped Ivy spread her legs apart and stepped back to look at her. Then he moved Ivy's hair out of the way and tied it in a ponytail. He placed his hands on her waist to position her but got distracted and began to flirt.

He took some ice from his glass of wine and placed it on Ivy's neck, watching as it melted and the water ran down her back, backside and down to her leg.

"Now I'm all wet," Ivy said, making both of them laugh.

"I'll take care of that," Justin said seductively.

He began to lick the trail of water off Ivy from her leg to her neck, she turned around once he reached her neck so they could kiss. They leaned back against the wall, forgetting all about the paint bottles they accidentally upended as they did so. Just as things began to heat up, the host walked over to the door and knocked.

"How are you guys doing in there?" she called out.

"Good!" Justin squealed, his voice coming out high-pitched and girly. Embarrassed, he buried his head in Ivy's shoulder and cleared his throat.

Ivy muffled her laughs, and Justin groaned.

"I mean, good. We're doing great," he said in his usual voice.

"Really? A girl's voice?" Ivy asked once the host moved away.

"I don't know. I got nervous!" Justin defended himself.

They laughed and then finished up their art.

"We made a mess. The paint is everywhere! What are we going to say?" Justin worried.

"Apologize and leave an extra tip," Ivy said wittily.

They exited the room and walked across the hall, glancing at the open doors and realizing that all the rooms were messy with paint, just like theirs.

They walked up to the front desk to pay with the others.

"Justin and Ivy," the body art host called out. "That will be $60 for two oil paintings and two canvases."

The host showed them their canvases, and they nodded in approval.

"Okay, and I want to pay extra. We kind of made a mess," Justin said apologetically.

"No worries, it's included in the price. It's expected," the host told them.

"Oh great! We made a mess, too," one of the women said.

"Us too," another woman said, gesturing toward her and her partner, and they all started laughing.

"$60 for two oil paintings. Two canvases," the host told the next couple, who gladly paid.

"That will be $100. Two oil paintings and three canvases," the body art host told the final couple.

Justin, Ivy and the other couple looked at each other.

"Three canvases?" Ivy mouthed silently, and Justin nodded, eyes widening comically.

"Yeah, we had to pay extra," the last couple said. The host nodded, handing them three canvases. It cost them more because of the couple's very enormous shapely figures.

They both snickered and quickly left the building, walking hand in hand and feeling very spirited. The gym was nearby, so they drove to the gym to get a quick workout in. Once there, Justin peeked his head into Ron's office while Ivy waited for him.

"I decided," Justin said excitedly. "Let me train Ivy first. I'll be right back."

"Okay," Ron said, nodding.

"What was that about?" Ivy asked as Justin took her hand, and they walked over to the cable machines.

"Nothing really," Justin said, training Ivy for the next thirty minutes.

"Great job today!" he complimented once they were done. "Go on the treadmill for a 15 min cool down while I speak to Ron."

"Okay," she said, hopping onto the treadmill. Tiffany and Veronica hopped onto the treadmills beside her, breaking off into light jogs.

Ivy watched curiously from afar as Justin conversed with Ron.

"After thinking about it, I'm going to have to stay. I've found something special in Ivy."

"Are you sure?" Ron asked.

"I'm sure," Justin said confidently, barely even hesitating.

Meanwhile, Tiffany and Veronica were side-eyeing Ivy as they jogged.

"That man is a great trainer," Veronica said loudly, gesturing to Justin, who had walked into Ron's office just then.

"Let me tell you, he's great in bed too," Tiffany added.

"Yes, girl," Tiffany cheered. "We just had a one-on-one session at his place not too long ago. Trust me when I say I burned more than my share of calories."

Both women started laughing, and Ivy's lip curled in disgust. She hopped off the treadmill, and the two women grinned when they saw her visible distress.

Justin was leaving Ron's office feeling content about his decision when he saw Ivy upset and walked toward her. She walked past him, ignoring him completely. He quickly jogged to catch up to her.

"What's wrong?" Justin asked, concerned.

"Go ask your little friend over there," Ivy spat without looking at him.

She pointed to Veronica and Tiffany, and Justin looked over to see them laughing. He dropped his head and sighed.

"So, it's true?" Ivy assumed.

"Let me explain," Justin insisted, but Ivy stormed toward the door.

"Wait, let me explain!" he shouted, catching up to her and blocking the doorway.

Ivy pushed against his chest to get him to move. "Too late for that!" she scoffed, pushing past him and leaving.

Justin stared at Tiffany; his eyebrows furrowed in anger and pain.

"Damn it!" he exclaimed.

Miguel, who was training a client, looked over and saw Tiffany laughing at the situation. He felt the strong urge to protect his friend but let Justin handle it.

Justin, on the other hand, let his anger get to him.

He strode over to Ron's office and declared, "I'll take that position. Just get me out of here."

Chapter 12: No More Ditto

Justin's therapist was sitting in his office; his day had come to an end. He gathered his paperwork from his desk and placed it in his briefcase. He glanced down at his phone as he scooped it to leave and paused, staring at the screen, hoping to hear from Justin. He was hopeful Justin finally spoke with his heart.

Ivy sat in her room, reflecting on her day. She could not stop thinking about the incident at the gym. It was extremely overwhelming for her. Eventually, she got up and prepared herself a hot bath. Her tears started falling as soon as she was submerged in the water.

On the other hand, Justin sat on his patio, sipping wine and listening to bachata.

One Month Later

One month later, Justin entered the gym and sighed. It looked exactly like the one in Ohio, but the sign on this door read 'Manager', but he still couldn't get used to it. Something seemed to be missing.

He had already notified the front desk and asked them to send him his first client.

There was a knock on his door.

"Come in," Justin said, and a tall, voluptuous woman walked in.

"Hello," she said, taking a seat.

"Hello," Justin replied, looking down at her file and reading her name on it. "So, Mrs. Lindsey. What are your fitness goals?"

"It's just Ms. Lindsey, with no r," she corrected.

"Oh, okay," Justin said. "I apologize, Ms. Lindsey."

"I'm trying to lose 20 pounds, and I would like to accentuate my hips and chest," she told him, gesturing to the areas of her body that needed work.

"Oohhh, okay," Justin said with a professional nod. "I think I can help."

"Okay, great!" she cheered.

"Let's just get you started with three times a week. Cardio five times a week, and I'll put together a meal plan for you," Justin said, jotting something down on a paper pad.

"Sounds good. Would you like to have dinner with me tonight?" Ms. Lindsey asked.

Justin raised his eyebrows. He hesitated before finally saying, "Yes, that would be fine."

They stood up and exited the office. On the way out, Justin received a call from his therapist, but he ignored it, silencing the ring while he held the door open for Ms. Lindsey.

Over the course of the month, he went on several dates with Ms. Lindsey and various other women while he trained his clients and managed the gym, but nothing seemed to work out. He truly missed Ivy.

Ending his day, sipping wine and playing bachata music was the only thing that felt right.

***

Ivy was gathering up her belongings and preparing for work when she got a call from Keisha.

"Hey, girl!" Keisha exclaimed. "How are you? I haven't seen you in weeks!"

"I'm doing okay," Ivy said. "Took a little time to reevaluate some things. I closed down my nutrition practice and took on a job working for The Cincinnati Bengals. It's a great job and has a lot of perks."

"Oh, that's great! Congrats on the new job, but I'm sorry that you had to close down your practice," Keisha said.

"Yeah," Ivy sighed. "Lots of memories. Anyway, how are you?"

"I'm fine," Keisha said brightly. "I lost a lot of weight."

"That's fantastic!" Ivy cheered.

"Thank you," Keisha responded.

Ivy looked through the papers, balancing the phone between her ear and shoulder.

"How's Miguel doing?" she asked.

"Well, he's been moping around. He misses his friend. I guess they got into it right before Justin left," Keisha told her.

Ivy's expression crumpled. She did not want to be reminded of Justin.

"Sorry to hear that," she said. "Well, Keisha, it was nice catching up with you. I have to head to work. I'll reach back out."

She was tired and truly did have to get to work.

"Okay girl, take care. Hope to see you soon!" Keisha said.

"You will," Ivy said determinedly. "I promise."

Ivy hurried to work and walked into her office. It had a plaque on the door that read 'Nutrition Consultant.' No sooner had she settled in when her first client walked in.

Once they had gotten the customary greetings out of the way, she got to work.

"Mr. Bixon, since you began this new healthier lifestyle do you feel lighter on your feet on the field?" she asked.

"Yes, but truth be told, I have a little extra incentive to be light on my feet. I have a big 400lbs lineman chasing after me," Mr. Bixon joked, but Ivy barely smiled.

"I see. That is an incentive to get moving. So, the nutrition plan isn't helping?" she wondered.

"Yes, it is. I'm just pulling your chain, Ivy," Mr. Bixon said, and Ivy finally let out an awkward laugh.

"Oh," she said.

"But on a side note, can we do another veggie besides broccoli? I'm just not a fan of it. I have a hard time eating them. As a kid, I was forced to eat them. I would hide them inside my cup, and sometimes my pants pocket and my pockets would be wet and smell awful. It was quite a dreadful experience. I can't get the smell out of my mind every time I eat them," Mr. Bixon elaborated.

"Okay," Ivy said. "It's a simple fix. You can try asparagus or cucumbers, or a combination of both. Do away with the broccoli."

Mr. Bixon nodded and said, "Thank you, Ivy. Cucumbers it is."

"Okay, great," Ivy said with a polite, professional smile that did not reach her eyes.

"See you later. Time for my pedicure," Mr. Bixon mumbled.

"See you next session," Ivy called out.

Mr. Bixon left Ivy's office and closed the door behind him. As soon as he was gone, Ivy let her head drop onto her desk, exhaustion overtaking her.

***

Justin and Miss Lindsey sat at the dinner table, an awkward silence stretching between them.

"So, how was your day?" Justin asked, trying to strike up a conversation.

"It was alright," Ms. Lindsey said without bothering to make eye contact with him, too busy devouring her food.

"Well, how was work?" Justin probed.

She shrugged and said, "It was alright."

Justin gritted his jaw in frustration. His eyes wandered around the restaurant. He saw a couple enter together and sit at the table across from him and Ms. Lindsey. They took off their coats, and he saw that they were wearing color coordinated outfits.

Justin turned to Ms. Lindsey. "Do you like Spanish food?" Justin asked.

"No, not really," she said shortly. "Not a fan of all the beans."

"Ah, okay," he replied, nodding his head.

He looked over at the opposite table and saw the couple laughing and talking. They were playing tic tac toe on napkins and playing thumb war, reminding Justin of the times he used to do the same with Ivy.

His phone rang, and his therapist's name appeared on the screen. He zoned out, thinking of his last conversation with his therapist.

"You okay?" Ms. Lindsey asked. "You're asking a lot of questions tonight."

Justin barely heard her till she repeated his name, and then he said, "Yeah, I'm good. Last question. Who's your favorite rap artist?"

"Tupac," Ms. Lindsey said.

Justin breathed a sigh of relief.

"Phew, okay good," he replied.

"But west coast Tupac-" Ms. Lindsey elaborated, and his smile fell. "Not east coast Tupac."

Justin's eyes widened, and he looked offended. He looked over at the couple at the next table, who had begun to share a kiss.

"I can't do this," he said, standing up. "This isn't me. I want someone to ask me about my day and how I'm feeling. In return, she tells me about hers and how her clients got on her nerves."

Ms. Lindsey looked stunned. She sat in silence as he placed his half of the bill on the table.

"This isn't it. I'm going home. Ohio that is," he said. He glanced at the table beside them and saw the woman wiping something off the man's lips. It increasingly made Justin more sure about his decision. He thought about how that could have been him and Ivy if only he hadn't been so foolish.

"Look, I messed up!" he said, turning to Ms. Lindsey and walking backward toward the entrance while he spoke.

"I'm in love! I am in love! I really love someone!"

He stood at the entrance and glared at Ms. Lindsey.

"And another thing. There wouldn't be any west coast Tupac without east coast Tupac. Embrace it!"

The cold wind whipped his face when he exited the restaurant, making him feel more alive than he had felt in years.

He picked up his phone, called his therapist, and said, "I'm sorry. I apologize for avoiding you. You did nothing but help me, and I need your help again. I messed up, and Ivy left me. What can I do to get her back?"

"I'm very happy to hear you apologize and express how you're feeling," the therapist said calmly. "And when it comes to Ivy, you already know what to do.

You have to do exactly what you're afraid of doing. Open yourself up to her. Stop hiding."

"Okay," Justin said nervously.

"You got this!" his therapist encouraged.

"Thank you," Justin breathed, suddenly making his decision. He hung up the phone and jogged to his car, making another call.

Ron was at the front desk, flirting with a member of the gym, when he got Justin's call.

"Ew, old cow," the gym member said, dismissing his efforts and walking off.

"This old cow likes to eat young grass," Ron muttered before picking up the phone. "Who Dey Fitness. How can I help you?"

"This is Justin. I'm sorry. I'm coming home, Ron. All I wanted was to be here with my best friend and be around beautiful women. Now, all I want is to be home with my best friend and be with the woman I love. I can't get her out of my head," Justin blurted through the phone.

"Well, you know, if you can't get someone out of your head, maybe you're supposed to be with them. Come on home. I'd already considered this. I could see you were in love. You just didn't know it yet," Ron said.

"Thank you. Can you do one more thing and put Miguel on the phone for me?" Justin asked.

Miguel was training Keisha when Ron looked over at him and yelled. "Miguel. Phone!"

Miguel jogged to the front desk and held the phone to his ear.

"This is Miguel," he said. "How can I help you?"

"It's Jay-" Justin began, but Miguel cut him off.

"Wha'chu want?" he demanded.

"I know you're busy. Just give me a sec. I'm sorry for clowning you for not coming with me. I put my insecurities on you, and that wasn't right. You've been my best friend since high school and always had my back when no one else did. I love you. You're my brother from another mother," Justin rambled.

"Te quiero mi amigo," Miguel replied.

"Listen, I'm coming home," Justin said quickly. "What's going on with Ivy?"

"Ivy closed down her nutritional practice and is now a nutritionist consultant for The Bengals," Miguel informed him.

"The Bengals?" Justin asked. "Really?!"

Then he continued to tell Miguel about his plan to get Ivy back. It was a long call that ended with Justin asking Miquel to take care of a few things for him.

"Done," Miguel said, and Justin hung up the phone. Miguel began to walk off, but Ron grasped his arm.

"That was a long call. What did he say?" Ron asked curiously.

"He apologized," Miguel told him.

"He's a good kid," Ron said with a nod of approval.

"He also said he is opening his own gym and wants me and Natalia to be his trainers," Miguel added.

Ron scowled, his tone and demeanor changing immediately.

"That mofo," he grunted. "I always hated that kid."

On the other side of the country, Justin called the property manager, remembering the place Ivy had once wanted to buy.

"I'm interested in the property located at 123 street," he said into the phone once his call was picked up.

"Yeah, um," the property manager said. "You have to place your bid online. We have a dozen bids on it already."

"This building is really important to me, sir," Justin insisted.

"I'm sorry, sir," the property manager apologized. "You must place your bid online. There's nothing I can do."

He hung up the phone, and Justin groaned, fighting the urge to punch something.

Next, he booked the earliest flight, packed up his belongings into suitcases, and boarded his flight. He had gotten himself a window seat so he wouldn't be bothered. He found himself sitting next to an old woman and her granddaughter.

Justin was in deep thought, smiling to himself, when the old woman noticed his giddy grin.

"Who is she?" the old woman asked, and when Justin didn't answer, she repeated her question. "Sir, who is she?"

"Who is she???" Justin asked, slightly confused. "I'm not sure who you are referring to."

"The lady you are reminiscing about. The one because of whom you can't wipe the smile off your face!" the old woman exclaimed.

"Her name is Ivy," Justin confided. "I haven't spoken to or seen her in months and left on bad terms. I'm going home, and I have to prove to her that I love her."

"So, you left on bad terms?" the old woman asked.

"Yes," Justin clarified.

"You haven't seen or spoken to her in months?" the old woman asked again.

Justin nodded. "Yes."

"Kiss her," she told him. "And I mean really kiss her."

"Kiss her?" Justin wondered. "I'm not a good kisser. I don't like to kiss."

"Well, maybe you haven't been with the right one. The kiss will speak volumes when you are with the right one," the old woman said wisely.

"I don't know," Justin mumbled.

"Trust me," she said, leaning closer. "The kiss will set you free, she insisted. "She will know you love her. I promise on my little black book."

She caressed Justin's face and then kissed him.

Justin stiffened in shock.

"Grandma!" the old woman's granddaughter exclaimed, scandalized.

"Oh, hush," she said. "I'm helping him."

"How did I do?" Justin wondered.

"Nah, that wasn't it, honey," she said politely.

"Okay, let me try again," Justin said. He gently caressed her face, leaned in, and kissed her.

"Now, that approach was everything," she said. "But the kiss, not so much."

Justin threw his head back on the seat, disappointed.

"I'm never going to convince her I truly love her," he said sadly.

"Yes, you will. That kiss wasn't meant for me. It's for her. So, when you kiss her, kiss with your heart, and she will feel it. She will melt into your arms," the old woman said encouragingly.

"Please fasten all seat belts. We'll be landing soon at Cincinnati/Kentucky international airport, and please stay seated if you have a connecting flight," the pilot called over the intercom, and Justin's posture became nervous.

"Thank you so much," he told the old woman, sitting up.

"No. Thank you. Good luck, and remember to kiss her from your heart," she said as the plane landed. Justin grabbed his things and started to leave.

"Okay, thanks again," he said as he exited the plane.

The old woman fixed her clothes and sighed in satisfaction.

"This is a nice way to travel," she said.

She looked across the aisle and saw another young man sitting by himself. She got up to join him.

"Who is she?" she asked him.

He looked over at her, and she bit her lip.

Justin saw the entire interaction and narrowed his eyes, shaking his head as he left. When he exited the airport, Miguel was already waiting for him. Justin hopped in and threw his stuff in the back seat.

"Thanks for picking me up, bro," Justin said, dabbing him up.

"No problem," Miguel told him. "How was the flight?"

"Cool," Justin commented with a grin. "I learned how to kiss."

Miguel shook his head and mumbled, "I'm not even going to ask."

"Don't," Justin insisted. "I need to make a call real quick."

"Go ahead," Miguel said, and Justin pulled out his phone, dialing a number he had already memorized.

The call was picked up.

"Hello?" a female voice called from the phone speakers, and Justin nervously wiped his palm on his jeans.

"Mom," he said, hesitating. "I just wanted to say I'm sorry. I love you, and I know you tried your best."

"Thank you," his mom said. "I love you. But you were right. I could've done better. I'm proud of you. You were able to see the cracks and brave enough to say you didn't want it for you."

Justin smiled, fighting away the tears that filled his eyes.

"This Ivy must be a really special person," his mom continued. "I hope to meet her."

"You will," Justin told her.

"I wish the best for you too. I love you," she said. It was the first time she had told him she loved him and fully meant it.

"I love you," Justin said, quickly blinking, looking up to prevent tears from falling as they hung up.

Miguel tapped his leg.

"Good shit," he said encouragingly.

Justin composed himself and asked, "Did you get in touch with Mr. Harris?"

"No," Miguel said.

"No?!" Justin demanded.

Miguel shrugged and said, "Bro, I got you. I wasn't able to get the Fasha, but I got Trey."

"Fasha?!" Justin asked.

"A pig in a blanket. A smoke and a pancake," Miguel said cryptically.

Justin threw his hands up in frustration.

"What?" he exclaimed.

"Austin Powers," Miguel said. "I was watching it before I picked you up."

"Bro, you got Trey's number, right?" Justin repeated.

"No," Miguel said again, and Justin scowled.

"No?" he demanded. "What do you mean?"

"I know where Trey is right now. He is at this skate park on the east side. He's a skateboard junkie," Miguel told him.

"Okay, let's hurry," Justin said, impatiently hitting the dashboard several times.

They reached the park and stood off to one side, watching skateboarders do tricks and looking around for Trey.

Music was playing, and Miguel couldn't help but dance along to it, just when they saw Trey grab his board. He performed some complex skateboard trick that raised a round of applause. Miguel and Justin clapped with the crowd before approaching him.

"Good trick!" Justin complimented.

"Thanks!" Trey said.

"I hear you're also a pretty good running back," Justin added.

"Yes, sir!" Trey said. "Now, who are you guys?"

"This is Miguel, and I'm Justin, the best trainer in the tri-state and the only person who can get you ready for the Combine," Justin said, pointing to himself.

"The best you say?" Trey asked. "Better than Tyrone Brown?"

"I'm better," Justin said with a confident shrug.

"How about trainer Reuben Shaw?" Trey asked.

Justin smirked and said, "I'm better."

"Byron Thompson?" Trey questioned, and Justin just pointed to himself.

"You know what?" Trey responded. "Enough talking. Let's get it in right now."

Justin raised his eyebrows, and Trey led him into an indoor training facility nearby. He quickly did his warmups, sweating as he did so, trying to prepare his body for Justin's demo workout.

"You got this," Miguel said, reassuringly touching Justin's shoulder.

"You ready?" Justin called out to Trey.

"Time to make the donuts," Trey said, removing his shirt. Justin took him through a series of drills for the next 30 minutes, and when it ended, Trey was hunched over, breathing heavily.

"Good workout, huh?" Justin asked, and Trey nodded.

"Nice session," he admitted. "But can you duplicate this for the next three months until the Combine?"

"Without a doubt," Justin reassured him.

"Okay, the job is yours," Trey said, dabbing him.

"I need one favor if you will," Justin implored.

Trey nodded and said, "Shoot."

"Your dad's phone number," Justin said, and Trey nodded.

Miguel drove them to a diner to get some food after the workout, and Justin thought about how he would convince Trey's dad. The three of them stood in line, ordering food, when Trey turned to Justin.

"Yo, I appreciate you guys treating me to lunch," Trey said.

"No problem at all," Justin replied. "I appreciate you calling your dad for me."

"No doubt," Trey said as they got their food and sat down. Trey called his father and waited for him to pick up.

"Dad? I found a trainer I want to work with for the Combine, and he's right here," he said into the phone.

"Okay, magnificent," his dad said. "Let me chat with him."

Trey offered the phone to Justin, and he took it.

"Hello sir, my name is Justin Jackson, and I am the top trainer" Justin began to say.

"I know who you are," Mr. Jackson, Trey's father, interrupted. "What is this going to cost me?"

"You know who I am?" Justin asked, raising a brow.

"Well, sure. I wouldn't be a good father if I didn't do my due diligence in finding the best trainer around in preparation for my son going to the next level. Word on the street is it's you. So, what is this going to cost me?" Mr. Harris pushed.

"Well, sir. I was kind of hoping you could help me with two things. The first being you and Trey letting people know who got him ready for the Combine," Justin said.

"And the second request?" Mr. Harris barked.

"I'm trying to purchase a building for my training facility, and the property manager is giving me a hard time. I understand that you are the owner of the property, and I was hoping you'd step in allowing me to purchase it. That way, my cost to you is pro bono," Justin replied.

"Say less," Mr. Harris said. He made another phone call and clicked over for a moment. He got back to Justin a few minutes later.

"It's yours to purchase."

"Thank you, sir, thank you so much!" Justin exclaimed.

"I expect my son to be in top-notch shape for the Combine. He's going to be the number one pick," Mr. Harris insisted.

"Yes, sir. Done," Justin said.

Three Weeks Later in Indiana

Before the opening of his new gym, Justin sat in the press box, looking on as Trey did his Combine drills on the field. He sat down a couple of seats behind the head coach of The Cincinnati Bengals.

"That Harris kid would look great in black and orange," Justin commented.

"Excuse me?" The Bengals coach asked.

"I was just saying how the projected number one pick, Trey Harris, would look good in black and orange. And how lucky you guys are to have the number one pick and he just happens to be a local kid," Justin said.

"So, they say number one," the coach said with a laugh, not turning around to acknowledge Justin.

"Yeah, but none the less I hear he wants to go out west, though," Justin elaborated.

"Out west?" the coach wondered.

"Yes, sir," Justin said. "It's warm out there."

The coach started laughing, still faced forward not acknowledging Justin. "How would you know?" he called.

"I'm his trainer," Justin informed him smugly.

The coach turned around quickly to look at Justin, eyebrows raised, understanding that he needed to take him seriously.

"Coach, I need a favor," Justin said.

A Week After The Combine

Justin, Miguel, and Keisha were adding the finishing touches around the new gym when Natalia and Jane walked up. Jane looked extremely good, with her hair and makeup done.

"Need a little help?" Natalia asked, looking around the place, impressed with what Justin had done to it. It looked every bit like the nutrition and fitness center Justin intended it to be.

"Yes, thanks," Justin said and glanced at Jane. "And Jane? You look great, by the way."

"Thank you," she said. "Also, I took your advice, and I stopped acting insecure. I stopped lurking around and watching her every movement. I know she loves me. But some good did come out of me being in the gym every day watching her. I am now a certified trainer."

"Wow, that's amazing! I guess lurking around in the gym paid off," Justin joked, and they all laughed.

"Aye. By the way, I saw what your ex, Tiffany, did to Ivy on your last day in the gym. That wasn't cool." Justin nodded his head in agreement.

"Well, let's just say I took care of her. I put itching powder on her shower towel. It wasn't pretty," Jane said with a smirk.

"Shut up!" Justin guffawed, giving her a high five. "Thank you."

"No problem," Jane told him. "You're family. And it's my way of saying thank you."

"I appreciate that. And I appreciate you guys coming out to help today. I don't know if you heard, but I need two amazing trainers, and I would love to add you and Natalia to the team if that's okay?" he asked.

"Yes, yes, and yes!" Jane exclaimed.

"Thank you, Justin!" Natalia agreed, nodding.

"No problem," he told them.

Keisha, who was on the phone, approached them with a panicked expression and said, "Ivy's getting close. You need to hide."

"What does Ivy think is going on?" Natalia wondered.

Keisha walked toward the front door and said, "A grand opening for a friend and a new gym for us to train."

Keisha ushered Natalia and Jane inside when she saw Ivy walking up the entrance steps and greeted her with a big hug.

"Hey, girl! Thanks for coming!" she squealed. "Just looking for a new gym to go to, and I wanted your opinion."

They both walked in and saw Miguel, who was arranging the flowers.

"Hello, Miguel!" Ivy said cheerfully.

"Hey, Ivy!" he replied.

She saw Jane and Natalia and made her way toward the center of the space, admiring all the decorations.

"This looks amazing!" she chirped. "This is exactly how I would have done mine."

She continued to walk around and stopped dead in her tracks when she saw a huge picture frame in a office with a sign on the wall that read:

"Make every moment count, take the time to reflect on what truly matters to you, and let your heart be your guide. Pursue your dreams and goals, and make the most of every moment. With determination and positivity, you can make your life amazing."

-Love, Mom

"How?" Ivy asked, tears filling her eyes and falling down her cheeks. "My mom wrote this before passing."

Justin walked out from where he had been hiding and raised his hands.

"I hope you like everything," he called out. "It's yours. It's ours."

Ivy turned to him; her face crumpled in confusion and surprise. "You hurt me," she told him.

"I know," Justin said apologetically. "I'm sorry. She didn't mean anything to me. That happened before we got to know one another."

"I don't know," Ivy said, staring blankly at him.

"Ivy, I missed you," he told her. "I know now that being goofy and silly with your best friend is okay. It's okay to wear corny matching outfits and hold hands and kiss in public."

He paused, hesitating, and then decided to continue trusting what he was feeling.

"I think about you all day. You make me smile. You make me want to be the best version of myself. I've never experienced anything close to how I feel about you. I let you eat off my plate, for god's sake!"

Ivy began to laugh, and Justin breathed a sigh of relief.

"Because of you, Ivy," he said, "I know how to reciprocate love and give it in return. I like when you call me daddy, and I want to call you mami. I wanna kiss and hug you when you're cooking. I want us to have pet names. And I know that finding someone to wake up to is better than finding someone to sleep with. From this moment, ditto is never coming out of my mouth again. Only te quiero, I love you!"

He gently held Ivy's face in his palms, leaning closer till his lips met her in an achingly sweet kiss. She deepened it, and everyone except them seemed to disappear.

When they broke away, everyone in the gym cheered and hooted, applause filling the air.

"I believe you," Ivy breathed, looking up at him. "I can feel you love me."

"I do," Justin admitted, touching her nose softly.

"Where'd you learn to kiss like that?" Ivy asked.

"Um," Justin said, deciding that some things needed to remain a secret. "You brought it out of me."

"Good answer," Ivy said firmly. "Don't upset me again."

Justin laughed and wrapped his arms around her.

"Never again," he agreed, and everyone laughed.

"I love the gym and my office, but I'm the nutritional consultant for The Bengals. I can't just leave. That would kill my career," Ivy told him.

"Yes, I know. I've already taken care of it," Justin assured her.

Epilogue

Justin's therapist sat on the couch, turning on the tv and preparing to watch the Red's game. His eyes widened when he saw Justin and Ivy on the jumbo cam embracing each other, locked in a passionate kiss. He nudged his young son sitting beside him, excitedly fiddling with the hem of his pajama shirt. His wife entered the room and hugged him, kissing his forehead.

"That's my guy," the therapist pointed out proudly, glad Justin had finally overcome his demons.

Justin, Ivy, Miguel, Keisha, Mr. Harris, Trey, and The Bengals Coach sat in the press box of The Great American Ball Park.

"I can't believe we're sitting in the press box watching the Red's play," Ivy said, leaning over and whispering into Justin's ear.

"Yes, unreal," Justin responded.

"Let me get this straight. They let me out of my contract and gave us these tickets for free?" Ivy asked.

"Yes, ma'am," Justin clarified. "Everyone is happy. Coach is chopping it up with Mr. Harris and Trey. Miguel and Keisha are happy, and I got my baby."

"Great job!," Ivy chirped. "I love you."

"I love you," Justin said.

They took off their jackets, revealing their matching t-shirts as they shared a kiss.

The End.